UNCOMMON FAVOR

THE INTENTIONAL LIFE OF A DISCIPLE

HEATHER JOHNSTON

Fedd Books
P.O. Box 341973
Austin, TX 78734
www.thefeddagency.com

Published in association with The Fedd Agency, Inc., a literary agency.

Cover Design by Deryn Pieterse

ISBN: 978-1-949784-72-5

eISBN: 978-1-949784-73-2

Library of Congress Number: 2021909282

Printed in the United States of America

First Edition 21 22 23 24 / 6 7 8 9

To David, Mallory, Payne, Joy, Lily, Henry,
and future grandchildren

CONTENTS

FOREWORD

In this book, Heather talks about chutzpah— audacity, boldness—and indeed, I can report it's a quality she has in abundance. She knows exactly what it's like to lead under high pressure, where her faith and warmth have stood tall through untold trials. Her strength as a woman and a disciple have been a personal gift to me, especially when circumstances around my own extended Mozambican family have grown most fiery.

Before being a stateswoman, Heather is a wife and a mother. It's something we share and deeply treasure. Seeking wisdom to influence a nation is a mighty and humbling thing, but first and foremost the kingdom of God is a family. The lessons we learn from true family inform everything else we do. We spend our lives inviting people to become sons and daughters of our Father in heaven. Raising natural and spiritual children, being a faithful child—these are dear things to God and the most wondrous images of discipleship. Heather testifies that when you lean simply into your Father's will and offer all that you have in prayer, you will be perpetually astonished at where He leads. Wherever you go, whatever you do, you can be sure that the life He offers is beyond anything you might predict. Even through unavoidable sufferings, it is more than we know how to ask or imagine.

The trials are very real. Each in our own nations, we stand every day in profound need of brighter light and deeper revelation. Heaven holds the keys of peace and justice, and in humility we ask for these things because the lost and dying children of the world need them. That is why you will cherish stories like the ones in this book, because now and always it is for Christ's disciples to intercede for those in need, to ask boldly for all that is required, and to receive His gifts with eternal gratitude.

—Heidi G. Baker, Ph.D.
Co-founder and Executive Chairman of the Board, Iris Global

INTRODUCTION

You and I have undoubtedly awakened into a new world—a seemingly apocalyptic one. It is not so much looming threats—like global warming, or the notion that polar bears could float away from the Arctic Circle on chunks of icebergs, or that an asteroid might collide with Earth, or that an ayatollah might soon hold the codes for a nuclear bomb—that keep sensitive people like me awake at night.

I am also not convinced that spirited protesters and global economic upheaval represent threats to our deepest core, although they are definitely rattling. No, many of us have come to the conclusion that evil has escalated in all of its ugliest forms—or at least it has been newly exposed to a monstrous degree. I am most certainly looking at a world I don't recognize through my kitchen window.

Small wonder that so many people feel burned out today. Our convulsing world has generated unprecedented discouragement and disillusionment, along with the belief that nothing is going to happen unless we make it happen, whether politically, relationally, or economically.

We need a radical review of what it means to be a disciple of Jesus. That is why I wrote this book. A true disciple does not convulse with the rest of the world. Disciples are far more proactive than that. The life of a disciple involves a risk-taking relationship with Jesus where time and again one moves through the human dilemma of helplessness into a wholehearted response to the Holy Spirit that gives the disciple power to influence their world. To change an individual and to change the world are not separate from one another, which helps us understand why Jesus concentrated His short earthly life on preparing individual disciples who, in turn, would lead others to know God deeply.

In the first century, to be asked by a rabbi to be his *talmid*, or disciple, was the greatest of all privileges. The decision was consequential. Following a well-known rabbi impacted your finances, your vocation, and whom you chose to marry. The decision was made quickly, though, because the privilege was great, positions were few, and you did not want to lose your opportunity. In the case of following Rabbi Jesus, the unforeseen happened. Everyone who made the calculated sacrifice to fully follow Him underwent a process of being radically changed into a powerful person.

Those of us who dare to follow Him closely today embark on the same life of uncommon favor and daily privilege. Jesus heals us deeply and then personally places His trust in us.

However, let's be real. Our setbacks and screw-ups comprise much of the journey, and there are days when it seems as if we can barely tie our shoes. Yet our problems are oftentimes our most optimal platform for courageous decision-making. My personal experience has been that when hurricane-type trials barrel toward us and rearrange life, it is not the time to stop and smell the roses or curl up into crone mode, even though these may feel like legitimate ideas. Our setbacks are often occasions when Jesus is saying to us, "Rome is burning. Drop your fiddle, change your life, and come to Me."

On a personal level, I have had serious health issues, and I have lived through agonizing mistakes that have impacted the people I love. I have felt more helpless than powerful much of the time, and whether it is right or wrong, I have found these struggles to be a good thing. Along the way, I've dropped illusions and dishonesties about who I thought I was, and clung tightly to the wild truth that I am deeply and irreversibly loved, as well as limited.

It has been risky to walk an uncharted canyon floor with my friends and family, but it has been worth it. I believe that together we have helped to positively shape a tiny corner of the world. The path of a disciple begins with personal honesty and humility that open the door to being conquered by God and reshaped by His powerful love. My hope is that the stories in the following chapters will be a source of clarification for your life. Even more, I pray they help you explore new territory within yourself and inspire your transforming journey to become a disciple of Jesus.

Glory to Him whose power, working in me, can do infinitely more than I could ask or imagine.[1]

1 | Ephesians 3:20–21, paraphrased

CHAPTER 1

CHUTZPAH

It's difficult, boss, very difficult. You need a touch
of folly to do it; folly, do you see? You have to
risk everything! One's head is a careful little
shopkeeper; it never risks all it has, always keeps
something in reserve.

—Zorba the Greek

Plato once stated, "The measure of a man is what he does with power." The manner in which we wield power uniquely reveals our character, and one attribute surpasses all others in its power to shape the world: *chutzpah*. In Hebrew, the word means "raw nerve driven by passion."

We see this chutzpah in Mary Magdalene. Once she realized that her sins had shrunk to the size of a molecule in the presence of God's mercy, she scandalously barged into Simon the Pharisee's dinner party and poured out her vial of Chanel No. 5 Parfum on Jesus' sandals, threw her hair forward, and intimately wiped His

1

feet. The Pharisees in the room snorted and sneered, and the disciples were shocked as Jesus announced, *"Let it be known through the ages that this woman prepared my body for burial."[2]*

Unapologetic, glorious chutzpah.

THE GIFT OF DISRUPTION

In 1997, Julia "Butterfly" Hill, an environmental activist, climbed a 180-foot redwood tree in Humboldt County, California, in protest of an invasive logging injunction. The logging companies thought to themselves, *This will be easy. Wait until it rains, and she will come scurrying down.* However, no such thing happened. Instead, Julia Hill settled in on her wooden platform at the top of her tree while sleet and snow fell, helicopters flew overhead, and loudspeakers threatened her with a jail sentence. For two years, her crew of friends used ropes to hoist meals up to her. Julia wore out the establishment, saw the injunction reversed, and saved the forest—and not just that forest, but hundreds of other forests around the world as people followed her story and her example.

Whatever season of life you are in, chutzpah is the agent that will bring change. If we stay where we are, where we are comfortable and safe, we die there. When we refuse to take risks but only accept what we have always known within familiar parameters, refusing to try new ideas, people, or concepts, we essentially fossilize and die. Change and disruption prepare us for new horizons, but only if we move forward and seize new opportunities.

SHAMELESS EXPECTATION

Jesus introduces us to the idea of chutzpah in one of my favorite parables. In Luke 11:5–8, Jesus tells about a group of rude relatives who arrive unannounced late at night at the home of their extended family. The family has settled in for the Sabbath and does not have enough food to feed their unexpected guests. The panicked host rushes to his best friend's house to ask for bread, only to find him asleep.

The desperate host bangs loudly on the door over and over again and awakens his close friend, who invites him into his house and says, "Take all the bread you need *and extra.*" There is no lecture, no complaining, no guilt trip—just "Take all you need *and more, just in case.*"

The context of the parable is important when we understand that the friend who was awakened represents God, who gives without measure *to the one who is certain that his request will be granted.* The man who came for bread is rewarded, not for his humility, but for his shameless expectation that he will get what he is asking for, even if it means offending his friend. Chutzpah.

Through this parable, Jesus reveals that chutzpah is the spiritual essence of an aggressive and passionate faith that pleases God. He praises those who demonstrate extreme tenacity in reaching out to Him for help. Chutzpah respectfully acknowledges one's lack, nothingness, and failure, while seizing upon the radical truth that God not only loves us but He knows us and likes us. True faith focuses on what God is like.

Rather than spending my time trying to get my act together and make myself presentable to God, I actually believe Him when He says, "Don't waste your time, honey. You are more beautiful than ever with those fine lines, wrinkles, and that potbelly. I love you like you are. If you're planning to ask Me for something, please come *believing*. Have some chutzpah."

As humans, we often hobble to church on emotional crutches, unable to throw off guilt and fear and stand up straight in true freedom as children of God. But we come anyway with the hope that even if we are in miserable shape, we can still be honest and say to Him, "I'm exhausted and discouraged, and I'm not sure I even like You anymore."

Would you be able to say this to God?

I understand why some of us are not naturally inclined to chutzpah. The attitude feels impolite, brazen, and arrogant. I have been around people with chutzpah, and they can be edgy and off-putting, especially at Walmart during a pandemic. However, according to Jesus' parable, getting our prayers answered doesn't result from timid and polite appeals. Rather, it comes from the deep conviction that we are esteemed children in God's house and that our Father will give us what we ask. Jesus links our chutzpah to our willingness to receive His good gifts, specifically *the Holy Spirit to those who ask him* (Luke 11:13).

This parable is not about persistence in prayer but insistence that God answer my prayer. Only if God is our Father do we dare approach Him in this manner. A daughter or son can make requests of their father that no one else can make, based on their intimate relationship with Him as the One who is loving, protecting, and providing. Extreme familiarity is the critical point Jesus is making, as a friend goes to a friend for bread late at night. Chutzpah.

For years, I was too gentle and timid in my relationship with God. I had a prayer life that resembled sitting with God over tea and crumpets, or a wishing ceremony where you throw your shiny pennies into a fountain. I possessed no theology whatsoever for being a daughter who could confidently bang on His door with my requests.

An effective prayer life, which Jesus explains is a primary credential of a disciple, requires chutzpah. Over time, I began to take His invitation seriously. As I entered into a more intimate relationship with Him, I understood His goodness and realized that He prefers courageous candor, even amid my sorely disappointing failures. In both the good and bad weather of life, He has asked primarily for one thing: that when I pray, I do so out of the deep awareness that I am His daughter.

A SUDDEN CHANGE OF WEATHER

After I met my husband, I came to understand the power of chutzpah on another level entirely. In 1984, Bruce Johnston came swinging into my life like Tarzan on a rope—tanned, fit, adventurous, risk-taking, and ready to save the dame. While he was enchanting, it was clear from the beginning that our dating life and marriage would be anything but conventional.

Our fourteen-year age gap was immediately evident in our music preferences, communication, and how we interpreted life experiences. Bruce was from California, which at the time seemed like a foreign country to me compared to the socially sensitive South, where words and manners matter to a high degree.

I met Bruce in the summer of 1984 while he was leading Second Wind, a high-adventure leadership program at JH Ranch. I don't remember ever speaking with him that summer, mainly because I developed a crush on him and didn't know what to say. Several years passed before we had a conversation, but I told God on the pages of my journal that I wanted to marry someone like Bruce.

When he came to Auburn University during my junior year, my friends put signs all over the walls of our dorm that read, "Heather is going to the Chi-Omega Formal with a 33-year-old man!" As an introvert, that about did me in. I skipped classes and crawled under my covers to deeply ponder whether going to the formal with Bruce was the right thing to do. Looking back, I'm not sure it was. Our date to the formal went up in flames, as I had anticipated. Bruce didn't know me or any of my friends, but more significantly, he didn't know how to dance, which was the main point of the formal. This was tragic, and it made me feel like we stood out even more.

I didn't hear from Bruce for a long time after that, but I was crazy about him, and when he finally called me, I was ready for the next step—which led to another—and another. As polar opposite as we seemed to be in some ways, Bruce and I discovered that we shared an irrepressible drive for adventure, motorcycles, and the exquisite beauty of the wilderness, mountains, and seaside. We are both romantics, and we love inspiration in its various forms. We were drawn to one another's spiritual lives: Bruce, pragmatic and purpose-driven; and me, a theological mystic and intercessor.

In 1996, almost ten years into our marriage, everything changed. We were unfulfilled by our spiritual lives, dissatisfied with our daily rituals, uninspired by sermons and Bible studies, and passionless about our future. We knew there had to be more than what we were experiencing.

Both Bruce and I had grown up in Bible-based churches and knew the Scriptures. Our livelihood was leading JH Ranch (the place where we first met), a guest ranch where people went for weeklong adventure retreats in search of their life's purpose. We had succeeded at leading people to great change in their lives. JH Ranch was a sought-after ministry where the Spirit of the Lord moved significantly. We were consistent, organized, and personally growing.

However, like a sudden change of weather, we went from sunshine to storms and became completely dissatisfied and disturbed. I can't explain what caused this—other than God provoked us to discontentment so that we would seek Him with all we had. In hindsight, I realize that there is a certain desperation that is necessary in order for chutzpah to arise from the human spirit and for change to occur.

WILDERNESS PURSUIT

Together, Bruce and I began to desperately seek God, banging on His door and insisting to know more of Him. Bruce began a forty-day juice and water fast, and I, in fine form, kept eating but dropped out of every activity; that is, I dropped out of every Bible study that I was teaching, every prayer meeting I was attending, and every appointment I had scheduled outside our home. In essence, I simulated a "wilderness experience" in my personal life where I only did essential tasks related to our two school-age children.

But I had to—*we* had to—stop our normal routine. Bruce and I knew something had to change. Our faces were set like flint for the adventure, and we had a certain holy nerve to believe change would come.

Neither of us knew exactly what we wanted to happen or whether we would recognize it when it occurred. Our thirst for God was the driving force, the center of our attention, and the total focus of our daily lives and conversation.

During this season, I had developed an expectancy about certain promises of Scripture, and I prayed aloud every day that they would become our reality. This was a strange but important time for us. Bruce was starving to death—literally. He was hungry and had become skin and bones, but he wasn't as hungry physically as he was spiritually. He was pleading with God to change us, to invade our lives, and to prepare us to touch the entire world.

Our prayers were filled with chutzpah—audacious, surreal expectation that God would use us to impact nations. This might sound like a far-flung appeal, but we didn't realize that it was. We wanted God to enlarge us on the inside and increase our influence in the world.

When God initiates a conquest, a love-impelled invasion into our lives, He overcomes our resistance, reduces our efforts, illuminates what is worthless, and apprehends our hearts until we are conquered. This is what happened to us. It sounds emotional and intense. It was.

OVERPOWERED RESISTANCE

Bruce's fast was coming to an end. On a January morning in 1997, I awoke late, threw bag lunches together for our children, David and Mallory, and scrambled to get them into the car. It was not a pleasant start to the day. On the way home, I was mulling over my failures: lousy mother, no to-do list, missing time with God, generally pathetic and helpless, and on and on. Self-criticism was my default whenever I thought I had failed or when things didn't go as I had planned. Pope Benedict XVI said, "Truth is vital, but without love, truth is unbearable." The personal truth I lived from was unbearable much of the time. This was the reason I had to experience change.

We were living in Rancho Bernardo at the time, near Lake Hodges, which hugs the chaparral-covered hills of northeastern San Diego County. As I rounded the lake that morning, the mist came over the mountain and the sun forced its way through the clouds. Suddenly, a voice penetrated my car, my thoughts, and my heart: *Heather, this is the moment I have been waiting for. I never want you to forget that I love you. You are Mine.*

I immediately knew that the presence of the Lord had invaded my Ford Explorer. I instantly felt like I had donned new clothes. In a moment, I had been delivered from guilt, fear, and powerlessness—permanently delivered.

Deep within me, I immediately understood that I was irreversibly loved, fully accepted, and undeservingly favored by God. I was aware that I was experiencing a supernatural invasion of God's love into my nature, personality, and spirit; I was baptized into a new mindset and new power by His love.

I could not stop crying and laughing. This continued intermittently for weeks. I came unglued, and it was strange—but I didn't care. I felt like the cheese had slid off my cracker, but I knew with certainty that I had undergone a holy deliverance from God Himself. A. W. Tozer explains it this way: "When He has overpowered our resistance, He binds us with cords of love and draws us to Himself. There, faint with His loveliness, we lie conquered."[3] I had to adjust to this new relationship with God.

---

3 | A. W. Tozer, *God's Pursuit of Man* (Chicago: Moody Publishers, 1950), 66.

COMING OF THE LIGHT

Soon after, I began to see into the spiritual realm in unmistakable ways. I had no tutors and no one to explain what was happening to me. No one had ever taught me or even mentioned that we could have visions like people did in the Bible.

I would awaken in the night and see Scripture emblazoned before me. The visions were startling and unmistakable, and with them, I had the keen ability to commit to memory the verses I was seeing. These occurrences became a permanent aspect of my life.

Some people might prefer that I leave these details out of my story in an effort to appeal to more people, sound more pedestrian and less intense, and provide a handrail into the spiritual life. However, I trust that this book has the right emphasis at the right time.

How else can we explain the desperation and chutzpah of the prophets, saints, and *talmidim* (disciples) of Jesus and call others to their lifestyle? How can we account for the amazing power in which they operated over countless generations if it were not for their hunger and their significant—and sometimes dramatic— personal experiences with God? Were not some encounters with God filled with terror, as when darkness fell on Abraham, when Moses hid his face because he was too fearful to look at God, or when Paul was blinded by a great light? Does the passing of time change how God relates to people? Are not Paul's era and today's era the same to Him? Is He not the same God, relating the same message to us today that He did to those of old? Does He not come near to those of us who must lay hold of Him?

Søren Kierkegaard, the well-known nineteenth-century Danish philosopher, said, "Without earnestness we have no essential reality."[4] That is, without intensity and shameless courage, our personal life with God is shallow and inauthentic. Earnestness deepens our understanding of Him and enables us to possess an intimate life of faith for ourselves. Yet in today's world of instantaneous communication, technological isolation, and mega-churches, our most authentic connection with God is easily swapped for five-minute devotions, secondhand opinions, and therapeutic messages.

Instead, we must cultivate the hidden personal life that Paul emphasized: *I have died, and my real life is hidden with Christ in God* (Colossians 3:3). In order to actually be Jesus' disciples, we must undergo a dramatic turning *to* Him and *away from* all else. The life of a talmid involves an unrivaled relationship with Jesus that is altogether out of the hands of men. Jesus leads talmidim into their own experiences with Him that are unique to everyone else's.

4 | Søren Kierkegaard, *Sickness unto Death*, vol. 19 of *The Essential Kierkegaard*, ed. Howard V. Hong and Edna H. Hong (Princeton, N.J.: Princeton University Press, 1978–2000), 148, 151, 213. Kierkegaard emphasized the word "earnestness" in his writings, by which he meant that to be a true Christian is to have death as the best teacher of earnestness. He explains, "Ah, we who still call ourselves Christians form the Christian point of view, are so pampered, so far from being what Christianity does require of those who call themselves Christians, dead to the world, that we have not any idea of what it means to be earnest."

In this season when the Holy Spirit came with such force into our lives, everything changed. Bruce, who is far more extroverted than I am, became as bold as a lion. Although he was bold before, he experienced an acceleration, an unequivocal certainty about who he was and what his message was. He spoke about the Holy Spirit without fear and with boldness. Bruce exuded joy and was unoffended when others were caught off guard by unique spiritual experiences in our meetings, such as people delivered from oppressive thoughts, released from addiction, healed physically, and other unexplainable encounters in God's presence.

While I went vertical during these months, Bruce went horizontal. He was eager for our staff, board members, and friends to understand the life-changing nature of our newfound relationship with the Holy Spirit. Our summer staff followed us in our thirst. I awoke early one morning at JH Ranch and went up to the lodge in the dark to find sixty or seventy of our college staff worshiping on their knees with their shoes off. This happened almost every day during the course of three months.

Some of those close to us were unable to appreciate the new context in which we found ourselves. Looking back, I can see that their responses were completely understandable, but those who were not offended by the unfamiliar and who pressed in with chutzpah to experience God also underwent a personal outpouring of His Spirit. When this happens, people are forever changed.

As talmidim, Jesus calls us away from concern about opinions, comparisons, and pleasing people, and into the deep satisfaction of knowing that He Himself is pleased with us. He separates us out in order to show us who we are in Him. Only our experiences *with Him* can change our nature, transform our thinking and values, and prepare us to be *sent by Him* with penetrating love and supernatural power into a world that is thirsting *for Him*.

CHAPTER 2

CHOSEN AND DISTINGUISHED

[A disciple] of Jesus leaves what is nailed down, obvious, and secure, and walks into the unknown without any rational explanation to justify the decision or to guarantee the future. Why? Because God has signaled the movement and offered His presence and promise.

—Brennan Manning

Light reveals us to ourselves, which isn't so great if we've gained another ten pounds and look like a mound of cottage cheese. But like sunflowers and daisies, we lean toward the light. Light creates warmth, and we want to follow it. Light enables us to see beyond the dark shadows into what is real, into what is far beyond us, as well as what is deep inside. There is something unsettling about the light of God shining brightly on us when He is choosing us. Things that once seemed logical we now call into question, and we are not so sure about the facts anymore. Things that were vitally important shrink to the size of an atom, and things that were insignificant suddenly shout for attention. The process of God choosing us can sometimes feel like being inside a washing machine on spin cycle.

CHOSEN

When God chooses us, Jesus comes and meets our great human need: to be singled out, identified with Him, and summoned. Nothing else matters when this happens.

As Bruce and I entered into that season, we knew we were receiving a personal call from Jesus to fully engage as His disciples; neither of us felt like a worthy candidate. In fact, the opposite was true. We were surprised by the tenderness, kindness, and power of His personal and affirming presence. God calls us because He loves us, not because He needs us. He calls us as we are, not as we think we should be. We were also astounded that His call would bring us into a relationship with Israel that would change our entire paradigm and view of the world—and ourselves.

For a reason I find strangely humorous, God chose to speak to me about Israel for the first time while I was in the kitchen. I rarely bake, so He probably thought, *This is a great opportunity. I'll entice Heather to bake more often by giving her a vision when she opens her oven door.* Fat chance. That didn't work.

Bruce was not at home that night, and I was baking cookies for our children. I reached into the oven, and Psalm 137:4–6 flashed before me in a vision. I grabbed my Bible and got on my knees as the verses remained suspended before me:

> How can we sing the songs of the Lord while in a foreign land? If I forget you, Jerusalem, may my right hand forget its skill, may my tongue cling to the roof of my mouth if I do not remember you, if I do not consider Jerusalem my highest joy.

I did not know how to respond to this experience or the verses in the vision except to say, *Whatever You need me to do, I will do it.* Then I ate the cookies and wondered why God was showing these verses to me in such a dramatic way.

Like most people, I had practiced the habit of spiritualizing verses about Israel for myself, which can be a positive practice. For instance, Harriet Tubman effectively laid personal claim to verses about Israel as "going up to Zion" as she ushered slaves over the Mason-Dixon Line.

Spiritualizing verses about Israel, however, can also be negative. A dangerous belief called Replacement Theology teaches that the church has supplanted Israel because the Jews forfeited their covenant with God when they rejected their Messiah. As a result of believing this two-thousand-year-old erroneous church doctrine, I thought that modern Israel held no relevance to me.

Consequently, this passage of Scripture bore relevance to me only in the spiritual realm—not in the natural realm or in this world. I later learned that it is a mistake to spiritualize Bible verses about Israel and apply them only to ourselves, since we then, obviously, dismiss Israel and her destiny and prophecies.

COURAGE TO STEP OUT

As God drew Bruce and me into an unusual season to learn about Israel, we met a South African pastor named Robert Mawire, whose influence felt like a tonic to my bewildered soul. Bruce had been attending his Bible study where healing miracles were taking place. Robert helped me understand the visions I was seeing and explained the importance of modern Israel in view of biblical prophecy. I was finally able to understand what I was seeing, and from that point on, my heart burned every morning when I awakened to visions of prophetic Bible passages about Israel.

A burning heart was not enough, though. I have observed many people with burning hearts and with dreams they long to realize who don't have the chutzpah to boldly move into the unknown. A burning heart cools off without courage. Bold moves are critical to passion. Talmidim (disciples) must discern the door God is opening and must courageously walk through, even if they do not yet see a clear path beyond, as I did not with Israel. Only in faith and obedience can dreams and destiny unfold. God affirms our courage with signs. I sensed deeply that I needed to do something, to move and not stand still.

One year later, I made my first trip to Israel, and Robert introduced Bruce and me to the leading mayor of Samaria, Ron Nachman. This friendship would become one of the most important of our lives.

In 1979, as one of the pioneers of the new State of Israel, Ron dropped two tents out of a helicopter, explored the undeveloped area, and then convinced a group of families to help him build a city called Ariel atop the rugged mountains of Samaria, only a short distance from where Joshua and Caleb are buried.[5] Ron walked the rocky terrain from boulder to boulder with his loyal followers and pointed to where the synagogue, kindergarten, and business park would be built someday. To this day, I have never met a more persistent and persuasive leader. The odds were against him every day of his life as he sought to carve a city out of the solid rock of this biblical land. He was deeply convinced of the importance of his mission—that he was pioneering the modern State of Israel brick by brick—and he made every sacrifice necessary to build the city of Ariel.

I did not know at this initial stage of our friendship that God would lead me to work closely with Ron for seven years building Israel's National Center for Leadership.

---

5 | The city of Ariel is partially Joshua's ancient city, the place he chose as his inheritance when the land was divided among the tribes of Israel. From a security perspective, this area was the most strategic landmark that Joshua could establish. The city sits at the height of the mountain range that runs parallel to the Jordan Valley on one side and the Mediterranean Sea on the other. Ron Nachman built the city of Ariel there for the same reason Joshua did.

VISION FOR THE NEED

Meanwhile, throughout the 1990s, Jews were pouring into Israel from the former Soviet Union with suitcases filled with their only remaining possessions. Ben Gurion Airport was overwhelmed with Russian Jews. The needs were particularly great at that time in Ariel. One morning at our hotel, I awoke into a vision of Jeremiah 31. The vision was about Jews "from the northern country" returning to Israel, specifically to Samaria, by a divine miracle. They would come blind, lame, young, and old. Women would come nursing at the breast or going into labor, and both men and women would sing and rejoice in their return.[6]

That same morning, a group of us who were in Israel together visited a small absorption center in Ariel that was packed with new Russian immigrants. My heart soared to see a cadre of Jewish Russian society in the room as represented in Jeremiah 31. In what would otherwise seem like a perfectly normal season to everyone else on Earth—a time when people were watching football games, driving carpools, and redecorating their houses—a major biblical prophecy was coming to the forefront with more than one million Jews streaming out of Russia, fulfilling numerous passages of

---

6 | Jeremiah 31:8-9: *See, I will bring them from the land of the north and gather them from the ends of the earth. Among them will be the blind and the lame, expectant mothers and women in labor; a great throng will return. They will come with weeping; they will pray as I bring them back. I will lead them beside streams of water on a level path where they will not stumble, because I am Israel's Father, and Ephraim is my firstborn son.*

Scripture.[7] I stood in awe of God in the airport that day. I could not believe He was allowing Bruce and me to witness and participate in the story of His people in such a personal way.

At the absorption center, a Russian immigrant choir began singing in both Hebrew and in broken English. Their final song rang out: "I come from Alabama with a banjo on my knee."

I immediately ducked down in my chair as if a large group of friends had unexpectedly started singing "Happy Birthday" to me. There was, of course, no one in the room from Alabama and no one who played the banjo—except for me. My dad used to take my sisters and me to Horse Pens 40 for bluegrass festivals, where the perfect array of hillbilly bands was always featured. In his enthusiasm, Dad signed me up for banjo lessons with the idea that if I could learn to pick "Foggy Mountain Breakdown" and my sister could learn to play the steel-stringed guitar, we would be well on our way to forming a band.

It didn't exactly work out the way he'd hoped, but this moment listening to the Russian choir sing "Oh! Susanna" was surreal. I felt like Peter and the disciples might have felt when they were personally called out by their Rabbi, except in this case it was Boris, the choir director. I hurried to the front of the room to talk with him.

Boris was a burly man with thick eyebrows and a jolly middle.

---

7 | Jeremiah 16:14–15: *However, the days are coming, declares the Lord, when men will no longer say, "As surely as the Lord lives, who brought the Israelites up out of Egypt," but will say, "As surely as the Lord lives, who brought the Israelites up out of the land of the north and out of all the countries where He banished them." For I will restore them to the land I gave their forefathers.*

We clicked immediately. He was uniquely passionate, and he intentionally sang louder than everyone else in the room, banging the old piano keys, standing and swaying as he played. He saw my enthusiasm and politely asked me if I wanted to join his choir.

"Of course I want to," I said, but I kindly declined and slinked away. As an introvert, I was surprised that I felt at home that day among a group of people I had never met before. I was dumbfounded not only by my experience but also by how precisely it dovetailed with my vision at the hotel about the Jews coming out of Russia and returning to Israel.[8]

NEW IDENTITY

The following day in Jerusalem was hot. Jet-lagged, I was leaning against a wall outside a small shop in the Jewish quarter when the shop owner came outside and spoke to me. "I feel like I am supposed to give this to you," he said as he handed me a ring with a Hebrew inscription.

I was shocked. Why would a total stranger give me a ring with an inscription? I asked him what the writing said. He smiled and said it was Psalm 137:4–6. He read, *How can we sing the songs of the Lord while in a foreign land? If I forget you, Jerusalem, may my right hand forget its skill. May my tongue cling to the roof of my mouth if I do not remember you, if I do not consider Jerusalem my highest joy.*

---

8 | The Old Testament prophets anticipated the return of the Jews from out of Russia and other northern countries, as well as from the four quarters of the earth. See, for example, Jeremiah 16:14 and Isaiah 43:5–6.

Something inside me awoke with a jerk, as if I had just been revived with smelling salts. I closed my eyes and listened as he repeated the verses. The verses that were inscribed in the ring were the same ones I had seen in the vision while baking cookies a year before. My legs started to go limp. I slid halfway down the wall and stared at him as if he were an angel.

As my back rested against the stone wall, my future crystallized. God spoke to me: "I'm calling you, Heather, to follow Me closely and know Me intimately. You will care for Israel for the rest of your life. I will give you My words so that you will know what to do."

When God calls us, He gives us a new identity. He separates us from the status quo and from the worthless things in our lives, and He prepares us to walk in absolute dependency on Him. Disciples of Jesus leave behind what is nailed down, routine and secure, and they follow Jesus into the unknown because God Himself initiates the move and offers His presence and promise.

When we give our whole life to Him, He unfolds the details we need along the way. This was Jesus' provision for His original disciples—for each of His talmidim. He prepared them and led them into His mission. He called them out, defined their identities, each unique and personal, and promised them the greatest gift of all: *Follow Me, and you will become like Me.*[9]

9 | Matthew 4:19, paraphrased

CHAPTER 3

BECOMING A TALMID

The task of the spiritual father (or rabbi) is not
to destroy a man's freedom, but to assist him to
see the truth for himself: not to suppress a man's
personality, but to enable him to discover himself,
to become who he really is.

—Nicholas Zernov

People tend to put pretty bows on scary things instead of just saying, "This is a nightmare. I'm going to hide in the garage until Tuesday." We live in a convulsing world where people who were once pursuing their dreams, believing they had life nailed down, now feel irrelevant, wandering, and panicked about the future.

And we have reason to feel panicked. Dangerous leaders are sitting at the helm of influential nations, and innocent people are suffering in increasingly disproportional ways. Any healthy, half-awake, sensitive person is pierced from time to time with the inequality and catastrophe of life for so many people on Earth.

IDENTITY EXCHANGE

As humans, we can better see the swing of life's pendulum when we get an intelligible view of where we are in the larger space of time and history. This context is valuable for us and keeps us from obsessing about temporal, small, self-centered stuff, which inevitably brings us to the end of a week, month, or year with clenched fists and regret. When we hook into a purpose larger than ourselves, we find the strength to survive the chaos life throws at us. As we exchange our fragile identity for the identity of a talmid (disciple) of Jesus, we become our true selves.

God spoke about the rise of modern Israel. He said that a generation would witness the fulfillment of biblical prophecies that have lain dormant for thousands of years. *Oh no,* you might be thinking. *She is going to write about the last days—or worse, the apocalypse!*

The truth is, I don't even remotely have the right personality for enduring the apocalypse huddled in a cave with stacks of bouillon cubes and evaporated milk. I have decided that I'm not sticking around for it, although a number of my friends are. They are hoarding Ramen noodles and Dinty Moore beef stew in their basements.

I, on the other hand, am captured by the here and now, by the way God is working presently in our world. *We* are the generation that Ezekiel and Isaiah foresaw—a unique people living in a particular sliver of time when the nation of Israel rises out of the ashes and receives God's favor among world nations. Our generation on Earth today is able to ascend the highest mountain to see what no other generation in history has ever seen or understood.

Only we are allowed to step into the unfolding story of modern Israel and its worldwide impact on all nations and people groups. Our generation today lives within a dynamic that is much greater than a small, myopic view of our world. In many ways we are like the first-century disciples, following Jesus and witnessing something entirely new happening in the world. If only more believers in Jesus could recognize this life-changing and world-changing truth!

THE CALL TO THE TALMID

Amazingly, it surprises many Christians that Jesus is inseparably linked to the Jewish people and their faith, and that to truly understand Him, we must love His people, His culture, and His religion. He honored most of the Jewish religious traditions of His day, including the structure for preparing disciples, or talmidim, and He implemented this structure when He chose His own talmidim.

When Bruce and I waded into deeper waters with God, we read books about the Jewish roots of the Christian faith, we asked questions, and more importantly, we spent years with Jewish friends. All of this deepened our knowledge of Rabbi Jesus. We celebrated Shabbat, Passover, and other Jewish holidays.

My decision to marry Bruce was unwittingly made in a manner similar to the choice of becoming a talmid. I was convinced he did not know that I existed during my first few summers at JH Ranch, but he insists he was observing me the whole time, which I think sounds a little shady. He and I went on one date before we got engaged, and then maybe one or two more dates before we got married. My bags were packed to move to California with him for the rest of my life, but I still couldn't speak to him without stammering. Our decision to marry sounds like an Evel Knievel jump across Snake Canyon. Although Bruce and I barely knew each other, like a young talmid, I had overwhelming peace about the person I was committing my life to, and I knew that the risk would be worth it. Looking back, I would not change a thing.

Bruce and I moved to California and lived in Newport Beach for the first year and a half of our marriage. I was a twenty-year-old who got pregnant eight months after our wedding and experienced terrible morning sickness and homesickness. I needed to eat steak and spaghetti by ten o'clock every morning, do or die. Thank God for the Spaghetti Factory down the street. By the end of my pregnancy, I looked like an olive on a toothpick—huge and skinny at the same time. It was not a look that inspired self-confidence.

On my way home one day, I noticed a group of fraternity guys on a balcony listening to Led Zeppelin. They didn't know I could hear them. As I passed, they pointed at me, laughed, and one of them said, "Have you ever seen anyone with such a huge stomach?"

I turned and ran back to our condominium, trying to get there before I burst into tears. I slammed the door behind me and plunged into despair. As I lay on the couch sobbing, the wind blew through a window and tossed around the papers that were on our kitchen table. The wind suddenly blew harder, and the pages of my Bible flittered back and forth, and then settled, open and still.

When I got up to look, the Bible stood open to Psalm 45. My eyes fell on one passage—Psalm 45:10–11: *Listen, daughter, and pay careful attention: Forget your people and your father's house. Let the king be enthralled by your beauty; honor him, for he is your lord.*

My heart stood still. The verses encapsulated every emotion I was feeling, as if someone had read my mind. God said everything I needed to hear in those two sentences: "Forget your homesickness, Heather. I asked you to leave your family and go with Bruce. I am enthralled with your beauty. I am all you need, so honor Me as your Lord."

As Psalm 45 continues, promises unfold, and they became my inheritance verses, as if God had written them personally to me. Thirty years later, I still live in the fulfillment of those promises.

A radical exchange happened that day in Newport Beach. I gave God my fears and insecurities, and He gave me deep and irrevocable assurance that I could trust Him, put my family in His hands, and allow Him, rather than my loved ones back home, to be my chief support. That day I stepped across a threshold into the life of a talmid, a disciple of Jesus.

BECOMING LIKE HIM

Jewish students in the first century who memorized the Torah (the first five books of the Old Testament) and excelled in their education applied to study under a famous rabbi. This required them to leave home and travel with their rabbi for a lengthy period of time.

A talmid was considered more than a student. The talmid's aim wasn't just to learn from the teacher but to become like him. The talmid was devoted to everything the rabbi said and did. The rabbi helped the talmid discover who they were and how they fit into a larger picture, similar to what happened to me when the wind turned the pages of my Bible and God validated who I was and what my future would be. People living within first-century Jewish culture understood that a relationship between a rabbi and a talmid was intensely personal and life-changing.[10] Both the talmid and the rabbi made a life-altering decision, and that decision was at least as serious as choosing a spouse. It included huge family implications that echoed for generations.

As Bruce and I chose each other in those early years (and continued to choose each other in the decades to come), we were led to make three life decisions that are integral for those who choose to follow Jesus as talmidim.

DECISION ONE: JESUS BEFORE PEOPLE

Jesus said, *If anyone comes to me and does not hate father and mother,*

---

10 | Lois Tverberg, *Listening to the Language of the Bible: Hearing It Through Jesus' Ears* (Holland, MI: En-Gedi Resource Center, 2004), 126.

wife and children, brothers and sisters—yes, even their own life—such a person cannot be my disciple (Luke 14:26). Restated, becoming a disciple of Jesus means that we are to love Him *above all human relationships*. Obviously, this verse is not about turning up our nose at or isolating ourselves from our relatives (except the crazy ones). The words reinforce the idea that our love for God must supersede our love for everyone else. If we can't make an internal shift about this priority, we end up holding on too tightly to the opinions of others. We cannot fear man and go with God.

That day in Newport Beach, I crossed a threshold. My homesickness disappeared, and my heart settled about where I was and who I was—and I knew that God had chosen me for this particular path. A talmid surrenders the significant people in their life to God.

DECISION TWO: JESUS BEFORE PURSUITS

Throughout my young adult life, I wanted to be a teacher. I prepared Bible studies, went to graduate school, and earned a master's degree in theology. I read great spiritual writers like A. W. Tozer, Brennan Manning, Bernard of Clairvaux, and Catherine of Siena. I kept notes and studied Scripture. I anticipated having a well-developed week-to-week teaching ministry, with Bible studies flowing out of me like a river. This dream must have gotten lost in translation on its way to heaven. But it was better that it did not work out.

It has been said that God cannot fully bless us until He has first conquered us.[11] This sounds scary to a sensitive person like

11 | A. W. Tozer, *The Pursuit of Man: The Divine Conquest* (Chicago: Moody Publishers, 2015), n.p.

me. I am not sure I need to be conquered—maybe persuaded very sweetly while getting my neck massaged—but conquered?

As seen in the book of Genesis, Jacob carried something hard and unconquered in his nature for two-thirds of his life. He stood at the ford of Jabbok as one whose only hope for the future seemed to lie in his own demise and surrender. Only after a humiliating defeat in his struggle with an angel did Jacob feel release from his willful strength through the power of God's conquest. The fight was long, but he became a new man. The stubborn, self-willed rebel was transformed into a humble and dignified friend of God.

We need real experiences with God that change us. We need a gracious invasion of His Spirit into our nature where we loosen our grip and gladly surrender our will to Him. And we need this surrender to happen over and over again in our life. Bruce and I knew that we wanted God's blessings more than we wanted what this world had to offer. In the life of a talmid, a decisive moment occurs when one yields all personal plans and pursuits to God. This opens the path to a fruitful life where God is clearly doing the leading.

John 12:25 says, *Those who love their life lose it, and those who hate their life in this world will keep it for eternal life* (NRSV). First-century talmidim surrendered every aspect of their lives: their worldview, career, resources, family, dreams, and expectations.

When we hand over our enchanting raisin-size dreams, He gives us an eternity-size vision and an invitation to join Him in changing the world. Every talmid experiences a decisive moment when they must surrender *all* to God. However, preparation is needed for a decision like this. We found it essential to carve out time, not unlike Jacob did through the night until daybreak. Bruce and I created a wilderness season in our lives where we sought Him and waited for the Holy Spirit to come and do the work in us that we could not do.

When you and I set aside time—a period of hours or days—we can construct an altar in our mind, our home, or our yard and say yes unconditionally to His plans for our life.

While it can feel shifty and risky to turn ourselves over to God, He rises to meet us in our small human-size offering to Him, and then He never forgets it. When we live a sacrificial life, we find God at the center of everything. He promises us an unbalanced return of blessing in exchange for courageous decision-making. We, as talmidim, receive the fullness of God's spiritual and earthly blessings and the wealth of His kingdom over the course of our lifetime. We simply cannot outgive God.

From my perspective, God took my dreams of being a teacher, which seemed wonderful, and gave me a vision and purpose beyond my ability to conceive. He took a shy, introverted girl who was afraid of her shadow, put her gifts to work inside a nation that was not her own, and placed her in a position of influence among some of the world's top leaders.

It sounds audacious. I squirm a bit to even write that. You would truly laugh if you knew how timid I was before this process unfolded in my life. If God can unlock my chutzpah, He can do the same for anyone.

People often wonder why this person or that appears to live in a slipstream of God's favor, protection, and guidance while their own prayers seem to go unanswered. It sounds unfair. The hard truth is that Jesus doesn't respond to everyone's prayers the same way. He consistently answers the prayers of those who order their priorities, decisions, and lifestyle in alignment with His priorities.

Jesus spoke exclusively with His talmidim, not with crowds of followers, when He explained the range of benefits for those who would intimately walk with Him. He told His talmidim privately that the Holy Spirit would come upon them with power and promised them exclusively that He would answer their prayers and give them what they asked for.

There are certain promises reserved for Jesus' talmidim: reward, revelation, friendship with God, and joy. [12] The life of a talmid is one of sacrifice and of ordering one's priorities with His. Unmistakably, His talmidim are the ones who have access to God's continual presence and joy, as well as consistent answers to their prayers.

DECISION THREE: JESUS BEFORE POSSESSIONS

Neither Bruce nor I will ever forget the weekend in January 1997 when Bruce returned from that fasting retreat I mentioned in

---

12 | Reward: see Mark 10:29–31; revelation: see John 14:21; friendship with God: see John 15:14–15; and joy: see John 15:9–11.

chapter 1. Bruce was very solemn when he walked in the house, put down his suitcase, and said he had to discuss something with me. He believed God was directing us to move to Dallas, Texas. When Bruce told me, I stared at him in shock. Had he really said a move to Dallas?

What he didn't know was that just days earlier, the Lord had said to me, "Go pack your attic. You are going to move to Dallas, Texas. You will own nothing, but I will give you everything."

As I mentioned in the last chapter, in 1997 Jews were pouring into Israel from Russia with only their suitcases, and housing was scarce. With great joy, Bruce and I gave the full value of a home that we were planning to purchase in California to the mayor of the city of Ariel to help provide for the needs of Russian immigrants flooding into Israel. Bruce and I were in a season when God was asking for everything, and we wanted Him to have everything.

We never felt that we needed to explain our decision to anyone; we simply walked out our decision in faith and contentment. I cannot express the many ways the breath of God was on our faces for the next fourteen years after we gave up our home. We lived in the treasure of His presence and provision.

Fourteen years later to the week from when we wrote our check to the city of Ariel, we walked into a new house that *had been given to us.* God spoke to the heart of a dear man who befriended our family. He humbly told me to choose the house of my preference in Birmingham, saying that he would pay for it, provide a decorator, and furnish the home for us. He told us to leave everything behind in our rental house—that all we needed to do was to bring our toothbrushes.

Jesus asks us to give our all, which includes yielding up our possessions. We often don't think of giving our all in terms of giving our homes or material wealth or comforts, but we do see this call in Scripture:

> *In the same way, those of you who do not give up everything you have cannot be my disciples.* (Luke 14:33)

> *Do not be afraid, little flock, for your Father has been pleased to give you the kingdom. Sell your possessions and give to the poor. Provide purses for yourselves that will not wear out, a treasure in heaven that will not be exhausted, where no thief comes near and no moth destroys. For where your treasure is, there your heart will also be.* (Luke 12:32–34)

As Jesus' disciples, we are asked to transfer ownership of all we have to Him. We also make a lifelong choice to follow His leading in financial decisions. Bruce and I set aside an evening in January 1997 and wrote out a second check, a larger one. This time it was to God. In the blank space, we wrote out the words "Everything we own," and we both signed it. It was symbolic, but it was real, and God believed us.

How small this transaction was in light of the responsibilities that God would entrust to my organization! One such responsibility (which we will touch on further in chapter 8) happened a decade later. Much to my surprise, God used us to help educate the US Congress on the missile defense weaponry of Israel and to see *billions of dollars* transfer from the United States to Israel in support of Israel's missile defense.

None of our sacrifices are worth mentioning in light of what He will accomplish in and through us. He has given us every reason to completely trust Him. We cannot outgive Him.

Jesus' talmidim walked beside Him and witnessed His miracles. They were in the boat when He calmed the sea. They drank His miracle wine. They had a deep, personal understanding of His unlimited power, love, and provision. When we exchange our life for His—our ordinariness for His greatness, our inadequacy for His strength, our limited minds for His unfathomable wisdom, and our human fickleness for His unfailing love—we fall, undone, at His feet. Nothing we give will ever be enough.

To be a talmid, though, we must first be willing to give God everything: people, pursuits, and possessions. Risky indeed. But we can also hear Jesus faithfully reassuring us, *Do not be afraid, little flock, for your Father has been pleased to give you the kingdom.*

Let our life of adventure, intimacy, partnership, provision, miracles, wonder, and fulfillment in Him begin.

CHAPTER 4

HIS YOKE IS EASY

> When we panic in the presence of our sin or the sin of others, it is evidence of how important the rules are to us. Our fearful response contradicts the message of Jesus. I can choose to protect the rules and create a religious culture, or I can choose to preserve my personal connection to His heart and create a culture of love and forgiveness toward others.
>
> —Danny Silk

Years ago, I made Bruce learn to dance, which was like teaching a zebra the rumba. Since then, he has evolved into a slightly lesser version of John Travolta in *Staying Alive*, and he spins me around to songs from the eighties or the Pink Martini radio station while we make dinner. We make time for each other, listen to each other, and seek rest for each other. We dress up once a week, light candles, eat hors d'oeuvres on the porch, watch the sunset, and then go to one of our favorite restaurants.

Bruce and I have lived a demanding, pioneering lifestyle. Over time, we have purposefully developed a rhythm that provides rest while strengthening our individual connections with God. While our rhythm isn't perfect, we have created a pattern that leans heavily on freedom and fun. Our busy working worlds, where we spill ourselves away, are allowed *only sometimes* into the sanctuary of our personal time together.

THE YOKE OF FREEDOM

More than anything, I have desired to live from a singleness of eye and heart—a central core where my outward and inward persons are at one with each other. My experience, along with the wisdom of others, has taught me that certain environments, lifestyles, and patterns of conduct are more conducive to sustaining inner and outer peace than others. Purposeless pursuits and fragmented living do not bring God's grace and power—they erode the soul. However, certain disciplines and choices lead to freedom.

The core of the rabbi-talmid relationship required each talmid to evaluate the rabbi's rhythms of life and rules of conduct. A rabbi's yoke encompassed his way of life, or interpretation of the Law, and application of his yoke to everyday living. Interpretations of the Law varied between rabbis, and some rabbis required more disciplined lifestyles than others.

A rabbi's yoke was the main consideration for a prospective first-century talmid (and still is for modern talmidim). They chose which rabbi they wanted to emulate based on whose yoke they wanted to adopt as their own. Similarly, a rabbi sought talmidim who were passionate about *their* yoke and who would, therefore, thrive under their teaching. If you were Rabbi Akiva, for example, and you were considering a new talmid, you would ask yourself, "Can this person take up my philosophy of life, do what I do, become like me, and perpetuate *my* yoke?"

The talmid asked similar questions. "How does this rabbi interpret the Law and apply it to his life? Can I follow Rabbi Akiva and take *his* yoke? Do I want to become like him and implement ⎯⎯ he does?" Eventually, a talmid became a teacher of the rabbi's ⎯⎯ absorbing his way of life. This process ensured that each rabbi's yoke was perpetuated for generations—even thousands of years.[13] The talmid had to fully believe in his rabbi's yoke, forsake all else, follow him, and *become like him* in all areas of life.

In Luke 6:40, Jesus says that every talmid (disciple) who is fully trained *will be like his teacher* (rabbi).

THE EASY YOKE

Not long into our marriage, Bruce and I came to the revolutionary conclusion that in order to effectively perpetuate Jesus' lifestyle and teachings, we needed to live under His yoke in our personal lives and marriage. When we hit rough seas and barely survived, we learned that unless we developed life-giving patterns of renewal, we would end up adrift from God and each other. Jesus said, *Come*

13 | Ray Vander Laan, "To Be a Talmid" (https://www.thattheworldmayknow.com/to-be-a-talmid).

to me, all you who are weary and burdened, and I will give you rest.
Take My yoke [my way of life, my interpretation of the law] upon you
and learn from me, for I am gentle and humble in heart, and you
will find rest for your souls. For my yoke is easy and my burden is light
(Matthew 11:28–30).

As our life and work developed, I dedicated myself to Israel
full-time, founding two organizations, while Bruce continued
developing JH Ranch and Outback. The Outback program
involves a life-changing weekend for parents and their teenagers,
similar to our programs at JH Ranch, but takes place in various
cities in the United States and in different nations around the
world. Separating our work lives was unwieldy at first, and quite
honestly, risky. We were both overloaded with job responsibilities
that spread in too many directions—the kind of pressure that typically erodes one's soul and closest relationships.

We faced our version of a line in the sand, but as we prayer-
fully forged ahead, we found more balanced footing under Jesus'
peaceful yoke. This required an attitude change in both of us, courageous decisions, and a mutual commitment to love and revere
one another.

Moving forward, our marriage developed like a strong tree
with a divided trunk and thick limbs. The healthy, separate
branches provided strength for the tree as a whole and contributed to its well-being and integrity. Bruce and I gained deeper
intimacy and connection, as well as gratitude for each other's gifts

and accomplishments, through healthy distance as we learned to see each other up against a wider sky. Our efforts enriched our marriage.

While I don't think they intentionally tried to make life difficult, first-century Pharisees and teachers of the Law often fragmented life for their talmidim by adding many extra laws to the Torah. Pharisees living at the time of Jesus were frequently regarded as inflexible with a long list of rules, similar to tough high school teachers.

But Jesus, the best-known of the first-century rabbis, condemned the Pharisees for destroying Torah. He told them that their additional laws created an intolerable burden that led to self-condemnation and despair. Jesus' counsel to the Pharisees' followers wasn't subtle: run for your lives or you will become like them!

Jesus plainly declared to His followers that He did not come to eliminate the Law but to fulfill it, that is, to explain the interpretation of the Law so that those trying to follow it could obey it.[14]

In the United States, we Southerners, regardless of age, race, or gender, esteem the many unspoken rules and cultural traditions that are ingrained into our lives. Those who grow up in the South know these rules and their interpretations, so they keep them without thought.

14 | Matthew 5:17. The passage continues: *For truly I tell you, until heaven and earth disappear, not the smallest letter, not the least stroke of a pen will by any means disappear from the Law until everything is accomplished* (Matthew 5:18). Jesus kept the whole of the law, both oral and written. The Bible testifies that He was *born under the law* (Galatians 4:4) and committed no sin. Furthermore, He was never charged by any of His opponents of breaking the written law.

It is easy for Southerners to spot "outsiders" because they tend to miss our cultural cues. Southerners are trained to be hospitable, kindhearted, and neighborly. We go out of our way to avoid speaking in ways that are curt or offensive. Men give up their seats, hold doors, and stand when a lady walks into the room. Toothpicks are never used in public. Small bites, straight backs, and one hand in your lap is expected while dining. A Southerner doesn't talk about bodily functions, even with one's spouse, except if someone is dying—and then with great discretion. Last but not least, when disaster strikes, bring food. Food is love.

Southerners subconsciously keep hundreds of rules and cultural traditions, so it is easy to understand that orthodox Jews also keep rules and traditions and adhere to a Torah-centered way of life that starts in early childhood. They keep 613 commandments and see life through their own unique lens. This Jewish way of life and application of the law of Moses is their yoke.

JESUS' YOKE IS UNIQUE

It was typical in the first century for a talmid to seek out the rabbi they most wanted to be like and whose yoke they wanted to follow.[15] However, in Jesus' case, the reverse scenario was true. Jesus sought His disciples one by one, pursuing those who would have been considered a "second-string" team.[16] They had learned their father's trade, unlike "national merit scholars" who had completed

15 | Luke 9:57

16 | Mark 3:13–19

Bet Midrash school and could decide which rabbi to follow. Jesus' team selection encourages non-Ivy Leaguers like me.

While Jesus did speak to multitudes, He spent most of His time away from crowds teaching His yoke to His talmidim, the select few who had left everything to follow His way of life and were preparing to pass it on to others. Jesus' yoke was unique from that of other rabbis and sages, and therefore drew a great deal of attention.[17]

His yoke differed in two significant ways. First, Jesus' way of life was about self-denial and uniquely seeking the success of others. He unveiled the largest portion of His yoke in His Sermon on the Mount. In this teaching, He envisions a heavenly kingdom of people on Earth who deeply love one another and renew their minds regarding what is true.[18] In this kingdom, the poor in spirit who cry out for a righteous life are blessed. The meek show mercy to their enemies and are blessed to see God and know His mysteries. The pure in heart hide their good deeds and serve God

---

17 | Matthew 11:28–30 clarifies: *Come to me, all you who are weary and burdened, and I will give you rest. Take my yoke [My interpretation of the law and My way of life] upon you and learn from me, for I am gentle and humble in heart, and you will find rest for your souls. For my yoke is easy and my burden is light.*

18 | The Essenes were a large ascetic Jewish sect in the first century who lived in communal life and were dedicated to daily baptism and charity toward others. They followed the oral traditions of the Old Testament. This sect was primarily located in the Dead Sea region and gained fame in modern times as a result of the discovery of an extensive group of religious documents, plus part of the Hebrew Bible, known as the Dead Sea Scrolls. The ancient Thanksgiving Scroll was found in 1946. Most of the famous Beatitudes from the Sermon on the Mount are found in this scroll, affirming that Jesus would have had common ground with this sect, enough so to incorporate their teachings.

in secret. Peacemakers forgive those who hurt them and seek the success of others.[19]

This radical teaching probably left many people wondering about their Facebook pages, their preoccupation with praise and position, their passion for public attention, and the propensity of leaders to strive to become popular heroes. Jesus' teaching caused His followers to rethink their motives, their relativistic attitudes, and their undisciplined thoughts.

"Can I really take *His* yoke?" His disciples must have initially wondered. "Can I follow *this* rabbi?" The answer was yes. The disciples desperately wanted to take His yoke. Jesus showed those who were following Him a new path to a holy and powerful way of life that lightened their burden. Those who followed Him experienced the holiness and power of His miracles and teaching as Jesus led them out of their sinful lives into new life.

Jesus' yoke seemingly required more from His disciples than the yoke the Pharisees required. Examples could be seen in numerous commands like, *You have heard that it was said, "You shall not commit adultery," but I tell you that anyone who looks at a woman lustfully has already committed adultery with her in his heart* (Matthew 5:27–28). Jesus asked for more than obedience to the Law.

In reality, Jesus was correcting the Pharisees' interpretation of the law of Moses. The easier yoke Jesus offered required a right heart and right actions that respected others. His yoke ultimately

19 | Matthew 5:3–4, 9

revealed a different way of life than what they had experienced before because Jesus' focus was not on keeping a set of rules but on a higher calling to a renewed mind. As John wrote, *Love not the world, neither the things that are in the world. If any man love the world, the love of the Father is not in him. For all that is of the world, the lust of the flesh, the lust of the eyes, and the pride of life, is not of the Father, but is of the world* (1 John 2:15–16 KJV).

THE PRIORITY OF A RENEWED MIND

Does not this higher calling to a renewed mind leave us to consider our primary point of focus—the Spirit's fire burning within? Is not the Holy Spirit our moral flame and our guide to a renewed mind and holy way of life?

While we may choose obedience, we will feel weighed down by rules and other yokes if God seems far off and unreachable. We are only safe when God's love is alive in our hearts because His loving fire empowers us. There comes a point when those who follow Jesus look past their questions because they are consumed with the desire to be filled with the Holy Spirit. This desire crowds out all else.

The Holy Spirit offers the way to live under Jesus' yoke while living in His peace. At some point, Jesus' disciples realized that they could have as much of God as they wanted. This revelation caused the apostle Paul to renounce his moralistic rule-keeping yoke to take the higher way of holiness: *I have been crucified with Christ. It is no longer I who live, but Christ is doing the living through me. The life I now live is by faith in the Son of God who loved me and gave Himself for me.*[20]

THE INBREAKING OF THE *MALCHUT SHEMAYIM*

Second, Jesus' yoke provided the platform for the inbreaking of the *Malchut Shemayim*, or kingdom of heaven.[21] In agreement with His Jewish contemporaries, Jesus linked the kingdom of heaven to Israel's story of redemption, both present and future.[22] He also went a big step further. He made the authoritative claim that the kingdom of heaven is here, it is now, and it is forcing its way.[23] Jesus was clear that He was His Father's representative of this kingdom.

Jesus reflected the kingdom of heaven in many ways: for example, the healing of the crippled man, the transformation in the heart of Zacchaeus, raising Lazarus from the dead, multiplying fish and bread, forgiving a prostitute, and turning water into wine.[24]

Jesus announced that His disciples were *entering the kingdom of God*, along with prostitutes and tax collectors of ill repute, and

20 | Galatians 2:20, paraphrased

21 | The kingdom of heaven is a fully Jewish concept and was taught by rabbis and teachers across the spectrum as God's redemptive power breaking into the human sphere. Jesus demonstrated that the kingdom of heaven is here and now.

22 | David Flusser, *Jewish Sources in Early Christianity* (Tel Aviv, Israel: Jewish Lights Publishing, 1996), 51.

23 | *And from the time John the Baptist began preaching until now, the Kingdom of Heaven has been forcefully advancing, and violent people are attacking it* (Matthew 11:12 NLT).

24 | The miracles, healings, teachings, and profound personal foretelling were understood by many Jews to be the *finger of God*. This is the same finger of God that delivered Israel from the plagues of Egypt (see Exodus 8:19) and that wrote the Ten Commandments on tablets of stone (see Exodus 31:18).

those whom He delivered.[25] In taking His yoke, His disciples made a calculated lifelong decision to participate in His redemptive mission to bring heaven to Earth. Jesus' yoke was indeed the yoke of the kingdom of heaven.

Jesus taught His disciples the primary prayer, *Let Thy kingdom come on the earth as it is in heaven.*[26] Once His talmidim understood that the kingdom of heaven is here and now, they changed their thinking. They watched Jesus closely and saw with their own eyes what heaven was like as it was brought to reality in impossible situations. Jesus showed His talmidim how the effects of the kingdom of heaven would be seen and felt through them and how they would facilitate opportunities for healing and destroy the works of the enemy in people's lives.[27]

A talmid of Jesus might pray, for example, to let heaven, where there is no sickness, be made manifest in a young man's life who is standing before them with a terminal illness. Jesus prepared His disciples to draw their understanding of God's will from the superior reality of heaven and "pray heaven down" to the earthly realm, where sin and darkness, sickness, disease, afflicting spirits, poverty and hate, and demonic influence can be redeemed.[28] He spoke of the kingdom of heaven as a reality that could be observed in the here and now with verifiable earthly results.

25 | Matthew 21:31

26 | Matthew 6:10, paraphrased

27 | Bill Johnson, *When Heaven Invades Earth* (Shippensburg, PA: Destiny Image Publishers, 2003), 38.

28 | Ibid.

GREAT EXPECTATIONS

As Bruce and I experienced the invasion of God's Spirit in our lives, we eagerly welcomed Him into the ministries of JH Ranch and JH Israel in such a way that we no longer just wished and hoped for miracles, but we learned to expect them and believe that God would do them. We realigned our minds to live in the reality that God is the same today as He was yesterday and that we can facilitate the divine activity of heaven wherever we are.

We knew we could not return to a one-dimensional teaching ministry that did not express the fullness of His kingdom and in which people were not afforded the opportunity for divine, personal breakthroughs at all levels of their lives. We began to understand from experience that Jesus is a miracle-working rabbi, the Messiah of the Most High God. Nothing is too difficult for Him.

A few years ago, a father attended our parent-teen program at JH Ranch with his son who suffered from autism. The longing on this father's face revealed his deep desire to have just one normal conversation with his son. His son's delayed speech and blank stare were noticeable, and those who shared the father and son's cabin sensed how isolating the disability felt to both father and son, especially inside the high-adventure setting of JH Ranch.

Day after day, this father watched other sons climb rope courses with their dads and laugh with other teens. He sat quietly next to his boy as groups of fathers and sons interacted at mealtimes and played at the lake. He noticed other sons respond to spiritual conversations and communicate with their dads on a range of teen subjects. This father's heart was uniquely tender, humble, and selfless toward his son, even though his boy was frustrated much of the time.

I noticed both dad and son under the big-top tent one evening when I was speaking about God's love. Our staff was praying in the chapel that night for a miracle for them, and other dads who had noticed this father's tenderness had joined to pray.

At the end of my message, I told a story about a modern-day prodigal son who had made his way across the United States after squandering his father's wealth and ruining his life with alcohol and drugs. I closed the story with a description of his father's inextinguishable love and how the father had lovingly shown that he would take his son back home just as he was and not as he should be.

Out of the corner of my eye, I saw the autistic son run and sit down on the hay bales at the front. His father followed him. Before long, tears were rolling down his dad's face. The son seemed to be responding to the message as if a window had been opened slightly and light was shining through.

The three of us got on our knees. The father was emotional as he told me that all he wanted was for his son to be healed. I asked the son why he had come forward to the hay bales, and he smiled and said, "Because God loves me."

BRINGING HEAVEN TO EARTH

The son's response was simple, but I'm convinced that his childlike faith and the prayers of his father and our staff brought heaven to Earth that night. As I prayed, the son was looking around. Other dads and sons were crowding the hay bales, waiting for prayer, but my gaze caught the son's as he fixed his eyes on me, and I saw something change. A minute later, I saw a vision that he would lead worship in his church and carry on highly functioning activities. I turned to his dad and told him what I had seen. I asked the son if he would like to lead worship at his church, and he nodded yes.

A few days later, the two left JH Ranch. The son began attending regular teen activities, joined the worship team in his church a year later, and after a few years graduated summa cum laude from the university their church had started. His father called me in the summer of 2020 to tell me that his son was getting married, and he asked if I would attend.

I watched as the son gave his wedding vows to a beautiful young woman who was madly in love with him. Later that night, I got on my knees and thanked God for bringing heaven to Earth in people's lives.

When we open the possibility for people to be healed or delivered from difficulty, powerful exchanges occur between heaven and Earth. Not only is a person healed, but God's presence changes the paradigm of everyone who witnesses the breakthrough. Am I saying that everyone gets healed on this side of heaven? No. But I am saying that the defining mark of Jesus and His talmidim is their facilitation of transformational experiences where people undergo needed supernatural breakthroughs in the presence of God. We set the table, but God, through the glory of His Holy Spirit, supplies the feast.

Jesus sent His disciples to duplicate what He had been doing. He said, *As you go, proclaim the message: "The kingdom of heaven has come near." Heal the sick, raise the dead, cleanse those who have leprosy, drive out demons. Freely you have received, freely give* (Matthew 10:7–8).

I have seen this command lived out with enormous diversity and joy. Courageous men and women have been called to the battlefield to break through social boundaries of language, culture, income, education, and literacy. Their authority is seen in their compassion and their willingness to call every human being a brother or sister. I have watched people who hold no political position bring changes to laws that brought sweeping justice inside of nations. I have seen healing prayers released over coworkers, friends, and family members with the expectation that God would restore and heal. Other individuals have spoken an affirming word at the right moment and have seen people set free from bondage.

Jesus' command means, "I am sending you out to do what I have been doing. Take My yoke upon you and also give it to others. Believe, and take courageous steps to release the kingdom of heaven in your sphere of influence."

It is easy to see why the disciples left everything to follow Jesus. They were in the presence of holiness. As they left their sinful lives behind to follow Him, they grew near to God and brought heaven to Earth. Jesus' yoke was freedom—not only for themselves, but also for others.

This is why Bruce and I yielded our insignificant lives to Him. We wanted everything His twelve disciples wanted: a rhythm and rule of conduct that brought peace, power, and His enablement to facilitate the kingdom of heaven on Earth on behalf of others. Like His talmidim, we made the decision to realign our lives, take His yoke, and renew our minds to not only follow Him but also to be like Him.

CHAPTER 5

A TOWEL

Only in a sacrificial life do we find
God at the center of everything.

—Dr. James Houston

Alone, we are doomed, but life teaches us that most people aren't easy to deal with, even the ones we love—*especially the ones we love*. People are edgy, damaged, and often inflexible, which can make relationships exhausting.

Sometimes it feels easier to be alone, to observe life from a distance with our own superior thoughts. But comfort and isolation are not where surprise and adventure lie. They are also not where hope is found, and ultimately, not where we find God. Change and renewal often happen when disparate people come together. God is an expert at bringing people together to create unforgettable paradigm changes. Ralph Waldo Emerson thinks along similar lines when he says, "People wish to be settled; only as they are unsettled is there any hope for them."[29]

THE TOWEL OF FORGIVENESS

The foot-washing episode the night before Jesus' death was likely unsettling, as we might imagine, especially if we picture ourselves in the sandals of Jesus' disciples. Several of my friends, staff members, and I decided to replicate this symbolic event, but when my turn came to have my feet washed, I cringed. The interaction felt far too intimate. Before I could say, "But I'm allergic to warm water," my friends had taken my socks off my feet, and I decided that every person present probably had huge issues they needed to forgive me for. Then, like an ice figure, I began to melt as I realized how much I loved everyone in the room and how much they loved me. That moment was holy and healing.

Amid the confusion and awkwardness of Passover night, Jesus created a jarring memory: with a towel on His arm, He dropped to His knees to wash the feet of those closest to Him and say, "I love you deeply, and I forgive you completely. To become like Me, to take My yoke, means to seek the success of each other. Get inside the skin of those on the journey with you. Know each other deeply—weaknesses, sins, and all. Make love your main focus, and keep your towel of forgiveness handy."

Jesus clarifies the role of foot-washing for His talmidim:

29 | Ralph Waldo Emerson, "Friendship," in *Self Reliance and Other Essays* (Mineola, NY: Dover Publications, 1993).

"Under My yoke, your joy will be found in walking the canyon floor with one another. There you are to take notice of and help one another. There is no room for competition, self-aggrandizement, or unforgiveness."

MONUMENTS TO AMBITION

For many years, I carried a fear of being deceived by personal ambition. I was brought up to believe that "the good life" is found in what we do for others, especially those less fortunate. In contrast, today's hyperfocus on political leaders, actors, clergy, and athletes as mythic-type heroes has made me wonder if our culture is careening off course into a science-fiction movie and that God might need to put the world in time-out. Today's culture makes it easier than ever to focus on dreams and goals centered around ourselves.

William Golding, the 1983 recipient of the Nobel Prize in Literature, portrays the tragic life of Jocelin in his book *The Spire*. Golding wrote the book in proximity to St. Mary's Cathedral in Salisbury, which has the tallest church spire in England.

Jocelin, the main character, is the medieval dean of the cathedral who decides that one spire is not enough; he needs to erect another. Master builder Roger Mason reminds Jocelin that the cathedral is built on top of a swamp, which was common in the Middle Ages. Mason is filled with anxiety about the dean's choice. "Please don't do it," he advises. "The foundation will not hold the weight of a second tower."

But the dean's persistence reveals his self-serving ambition. Digging the foundation for a second tower was like opening a cellar to his own selfish life.

In hindsight, the dean writes, "I thought I was chosen; a spiritual man, loving above all; and that I was given a specific work to do by God. But now I have insurmountable debts, a deserted church, and much discord. I do not know myself anymore. . . . I have put work before everything."

Only with pure hearts can we see God and discern reality. At the end of his life, the tower Jocelin had envisioned as a symbol of devotion became a deserted monument to his willful heart and led to a spectacular fall. God's tendency is to bring good out of wreckage, yet Jocelin would have to endure a long upward climb before being trusted by society again.

PICKING UP THE TOWEL

I put myself into my own time-out after reading *The Spire* in my thirties. I had remarkable ideas about how to help the nation of Israel. Reading the book cooled my visions of grandeur and brought me back to Earth. I did not want to create a path of my own making toward a spectacular fall. I wanted authenticity, compassion, and a towel in my hand for others. I wanted my way forward to be blessed with the kiss of God under the yoke of His intimate leading.

These thoughts were reinforced the first time I stayed in the home of Mayor Ron Nachman and his wife, Dorit, in the city of

Ariel, Israel. It was December 2002, and I felt like I had entered a shrine for God—a womb for the nation of Israel and her unfolding prophecies. I knew Ron and Dorit's humble lives were lived on holy ground. I asked God to help me walk carefully and to be relevant to what they needed. I literally picked up a towel in their bathroom, put it over my arm, and said aloud, "God, I'm here to serve."

God showed me how much He loved them, and He gave me deep love for them too. Ron, Dorit, and their four daughters had moved from Tel Aviv to the barren mountains of Samaria under the direction of Ariel Sharon, the famous war hero who became prime minister of Israel. Israel's peace treaty with Egypt had resulted in Israel giving up the Sinai Peninsula in 1979, and the wizened defense strategists at the time understood Ron Nachman to be Israel's best candidate to secure the area of Samaria as Israel's strategic security front in the middle of the country.

In 1979, Ron's family and a group of other families moved into a caravan of trailers in Ariel, where they shared a generator and drank potable water for years. Their community was similar to a kibbutz, a collective community that works together to sustain daily life. This is how the pioneers of Israel began their arduous journey.

Their later home was typical of that of the early settlers and of most of Israel's homes today: small bedrooms, efficient kitchens, and no frills—just everything needed for vibrant pioneering, including good cigars, canned tomatoes, and homemade jams and soups. Ron created a mushroom distillery in his kitchen for making kombucha tea long before it became popular, and he had a greenhouse filled with 260 orchid varieties from around the world. He spent his spare minutes gently caring for his orchids like they were newborn babies.

The most important meetings for Samaria were held in their home. Dorit, a chef par excellence, would whip up four or five meat dishes surrounded by a plethora of Mediterranean salads. If good eatin' makes for a better meetin', their home was the place. Crucial history-making decisions for Israel were made in their living room amid smoking, laughing, arguing, chutzpah, and mud coffee.

Bruce and I felt uncertain of our roles in the beginning, but we prayed audacious, faith-filled prayers about how to help the city of Ariel. We considered the emotional needs of the new immigrants and their families who lived in the city. When you are starting over and trying to build a new life from scratch, your soul often ends up last on your list. Among other things, we raised money to build a radio station for the residents of Ariel. It was typical in pioneering days that every gift contributed to a functional purpose.

In September 2000, only days after the radio station was completed, the intifada broke out between the Palestinians and Israelis. It continued for years. Israelis living in Samaria were now warned by radio about uprisings near the Palestinian villages that dotted the two-lane highway to Tel Aviv and Jerusalem.

REFUSING TO WITHHOLD LOVE

Little by little, we built trust. We got to know people within the Ariel community, and we loved them more with each passing day.

Bruce convinced Ron to send a number of high school delegations through our Second Wind program at JH Ranch—a two-week adventure leadership program in the United States. A great exchange began. Christians and Jews experienced a slice of life together that included white-water rafting, wilderness treks, and gathering in the evenings to talk about life's most important questions. We brought our college staff to Israel, and they stayed in the homes of Israeli students who had been to JH Ranch. Friendships developed organically and with great mutual respect. Because the relationship was such a happy adventure, we have continued the program for decades.

However, after eight years of friendship, things went south for a little while. I believed that the Lord had repeatedly shown me an idea to bring to Ron Nachman about building a JH Ranch in his city, but the vision felt unrefined and risky. Over and over again I thought, *Why launch into something new when everyone is so happy?* The last thing the Nachmans needed was a distraction. As awesome as the vision was, I was afraid of it, so I prayed about it for about six months.

It was clear to me that the nation of Israel needed to move toward its biblical, spiritual identity and away from secularism, which is the absence of God. How could Israel rise to her destiny as a light to all nations if she was not connected personally to God and her long history with Him? Secularism provides no transformational answers for life's crucial human, spiritual questions. I sensed that Ron Nachman would be a choice leader to open opportunities for the nation to discover how to relate to God in a more personal way.

After dinner one evening in 2006, Ron was watching the news while smoking a cigar in their small den. I asked if I could speak with him for a few minutes, and I laid out the vision for a JH Ranch in Ariel, explaining how bringing leadership training to the hills of Samaria could influence the nation. The vision was vague, but I felt strong, peaceful, and confident about what I was sharing. Ron looked at me, puffed some smoke, and said, "I don't think that will work here." Then he turned up the television.

I couldn't believe it. I slinked away like a child who had been slapped on the hand for asking if I could do the dishes. I thought I had heard from God, but now I was disillusioned and embarrassed. The experience reminded me of how King David, with every right motive, sought to bring the ark of God into Jerusalem from the home of Obed-Edom. In anger, the Lord struck down Uzzah, who reached to steady the ark, and all who were watching shrunk back in fear. David was humiliated, angry, and disillusioned because he had felt sure he had heard from God. Months and months went by, and finally God corrected David's procedure: only priests were allowed to carry the ark of God.

It seems as if there are two parts to God's will: *what* He wants and *how* He wants it done. This can make us feel schizophrenic, but we very much need to understand both parts before launching a vision that impacts others. God expanded David's vision to another level by showing him how to set up the priesthood for the temple. In the end, it was a win for David and for Israel.

I didn't recover quickly from Ron's response and I didn't want to bother him further. Forgiving people is difficult at times, especially when they have no idea how their reaction impacted you. Like foot-washing, forgiveness takes courage, initiative, and the choice to not withhold love. It is the only way to protect relationships and fulfill destiny together. It took almost eight months for me to realize my mistake. Why would Ron want to import JH Ranch into his city from the United States? Why would any Israeli mayor want to do that, regardless of how transformational the program was? No one would.

SEEKING THE SUCCESS OF THE OTHER

My second approach was scarier, but I called Ron on the phone this time. My whole proposition changed, and the vision was well-endowed. I asked Ron about the idea of partnering to build a national leadership center for Israel in his city (not a JH Ranch), suggesting that we could work together with Israel's Ministry of Education to create content based on Israel's biblical identity.

I told Ron that his personal legacy could expand far beyond building a city to preparing a new generation of leaders for Israel who understood their biblical, spiritual identity. I explained how we could persuade the major entities of Israeli society and youth to come to his city for leadership training. Finally, I invited him to JH Ranch to bring educators and city council members to experience for themselves a prototype for what this vision might entail.

The other end of the phone was silent. Then he said, "That's brilliant," and off we went into the wild blue yonder. It wasn't all downhill sledding after that, but what was clearly off the table was the notion that we would be importing our vision for leadership development from the United States. Instead, it would be a well-coordinated, combined effort; most importantly, his city would become the flagship for leadership training for the nation of Israel.

I now understood what Jesus meant in calling His disciples to seek the success of the other. Our organization would be hidden, and the city of Ariel would lay claim to an excellent program that we would help them develop. We would purchase all of the elements for a national leadership site and would devise the safety structure, which was our expertise, and the city of Ariel would host the nation at a world-class leadership center that would be incomparable to anything in the Middle East. Our benefit would be partnering with some of our favorite people in impacting the nation. This is exactly what unfolded, and nothing could have made me happier. Like David, I could see what God wanted and how He wanted it done.

Ron Nachman did not waste time. He came to JH Ranch in California in the summer of 2006 with his city council members and leaders of Israel's Ministry of Education. It felt like we experienced the clashing of cymbals over a long-awaited destiny.

Jeremiah, the wild prophet, understood from his prison cell that the invading gentile forces of Babylon would soon sack Jerusalem. To encourage him, God gave him a window into the future. Jeremiah saw gentile believers (*natzrim*) standing on the hills of Samaria—with an understanding of Israel's future and whom God had sent to support the Jewish people once they had returned from the four corners of the earth.[30] These gentiles would be sent to affirm Israel's Jewish identity.

I don't know how to explain it, but I knew this particular prophecy about the gentiles in Jeremiah 31 was instinctively ours to pursue. We were ready to do our part, pick up the towel, and serve the Jewish people from a mountaintop in Samaria.

Ron and his city council members climbed on our high-ropes courses at JH Ranch with only mild cursing and ranting. After a full week, we had formed a bond. Overcoming fears and challenges together transforms distant friends into family members.

Ron took notice of all that JH Ranch offered, and at the end of the week, he said, "I want everything that is here—everything. Would you please help us build this in Israel? I want the content, the staff, the training—I want it all!"

PARTNERS IN PURPOSE

We shook hands across a wooden picnic table on 7/7/07 and agreed

30 | Jeremiah 31:5–8

together to build Israel's National Leadership Center and prepare a generation of young Jews and Arabs to walk in their spiritual identity. The plan was a victory.

God brings unlikely relationships together, in this case Jews and Christians to pioneer a leadership center in Israel from the ground up and to establish specific platforms for impacting communities, cities, and nations. We sensed that this is what was happening.

Things moved fast, as well as slowly. Ron chose a piece of land in Ariel that he called "The Forest," but the trees were half the size of a man, so Bruce and I secretly called them shrubs. How can you build high-ropes courses and climbing walls above elfin trees that peak out at your shoulders? We prayed about everything, especially the trees, and we brought our friends to see the property.

The prophet Ezekiel wrote specifically about the mountains of Israel, the area called Judea and Samaria, where most of the Old Testament took place. God told Ezekiel to do some pretty weird things—intercessory acts that depicted not only their captivity but also the return of the Jews to Israel. One day God told Ezekiel to speak to the trees on the mountains of Samaria as if they were like people and to tell them, *Shoot out your branches, and yield your fruit to my people Israel; for they shall soon come home* (Ezekiel 36:8 NRSV).

We clung to this prophecy and asked God to grow the trees. Six months later, as I drove into Ariel with a group of people, I noticed that the trees had grown—not just a little bit, but they had doubled in size. I didn't say anything at first because proclaiming things like this could get you thrown into the looney bin.

I had lunch with the city manager that day, and she brought up the subject of the trees growing after we prayed. She commented, "We have not touched the trees. They simply grew about five or six meters over the last six months." We went to the top of the property to get a better look. Noticeably, the tree line of the property of the National Leadership Center was much taller than the trees outside the property line. This was a sign to all of us from God to start building.

God lets us experience the weaknesses of others and see large, complex problems when He plans to bring about transformational change, and He wants us to help facilitate it. A talmid is an intercessor in the truest sense of the word. They stand between heaven and Earth to discover the heart of God in particular situations and to pray His will into reality. Like Daniel, they come to the king with solutions. With an invisible towel on their arm, a talmid forgives where necessary, seeks the success of others, and walks beside them during tough times. A talmid does not give up on people, and this is a primary reason why God places His trust in them and partners with them in His purposes for the world.

CHAPTER 6

LECH, LECHAH— GO, YOU

Go. Leave your country, your people and your
father's house and go to the land I will show you.

—Genesis 12:3, paraphrased

Retired US Marine Corps Four-Star General Charles Krulak, my good friend, says, "You can pretend to care, but you can't pretend to be there. You have to go. You have to show up." He would know. With his compassionate heart, he followed God and protected the people serving under him in the line of duty. He served in the Vietnam War, where he was shot twice and was awarded the Silver Star for his sacrificial leadership in combat. He earned two Purple Hearts for his injuries, and he later led in Iraq during Operation Desert Storm. Altogether, he was awarded three

Bronze Stars for his valor and heroism in battle. He cared *and* he was there, and he is still showing up with a high level of visibility for marines who need his help.

THE JOBS IN FRONT OF US

Most of us have figured out that we must do the jobs that are right in front of us. We take care of babies, we work to close business deals, we sell houses, or we perform surgeries. Our work is sacrosanct and necessary, but we also realize that the world is hurting, so we show up and volunteer. We visit people in the hospital, pray for the sick, organize food drives, look for ways to help people, and bring God's kingdom into impossible situations.

I'm doing today exactly what I was doing thirty years ago. I'm following a person—Jesus. I'm not following a vocation, a vision, a good idea, or even a calling. I'm following Him. I show up for Him. I'm present for His assignments and for people. It has been pretty straightforward. I'm not trying to figure out what I'm going to do with my life, because He decides those matters. At the end of the day, I cannot improve upon His plans, although I admit that I sometimes think I can.

In 2009, just after we had begun to build the National Leadership Center in Ariel, I awoke during the night and heard the Lord say, "Lead the US Congress through Judea and Samaria." I was in between awake and asleep, and I thought, *Can You repeat that please? I thought You might have said, "Lead the Congress through Judea and Samaria."*

Night after night, I heard this startling sentence in a soft but audible voice. This statement, of course, was unreasonable. I had never met a congressperson before, nor had I been involved in politics outside of watching Ron Nachman make political decisions with other leaders inside his home in Samaria. I let the message flap in the wind for at least a year, thinking it might snap free and blow away. Then suddenly I heard it stronger than ever.

GO, YOU!

Sometimes we have to start with a blank page and no sense of direction, like Abraham when God said to him, *Lech, lecha!*—or "Go, you!" Yet God provided Abraham no direction until he actually packed up his belongings and began to move.

I hate when that happens. It is much easier and more reassuring to pick up where someone else has left off and already succeeded and follow in that person's steps.

When people ask me about a book they feel led to write, or a change to another job they are longing for, I always encourage them to do the research, ante up, take baby steps, and do their part. God doesn't do the work for us. Life tells us that positive outcomes do not just drop into our laps.

So it is not surprising that as I researched government-sponsored tours through Judea and Samaria, I discovered they were illegal. Glad I checked. Imagine me explaining to my mother, "Well, you know, Mom, federal prison isn't the end of the world.

Things like this sometimes happen when people are trying to do the right thing."

It is true—government-sponsored trips to that part of Israel were illegal. The US State Department policy at the time prohibited US officials from visiting the Jewish communities of Judea and Samaria, known as the West Bank. This area was, and still is, in dispute between the Israelis and the Palestinians, resulting in what we know as the Israeli/Palestinian conflict. The only exception was that people could lead privately sponsored tours there that were not funded by the government.

No wonder congressional members had never been through Judea and Samaria (the West Bank). No one had started private tours into this area! The US had been brokering the peace process between the Palestinians and Israelis for decades, yet Congress was not allowed to visit this disputed land that was at the center of the peace process. This didn't make sense, so I investigated further. Everything I researched revealed the same result: no official US trips were allowed into the Jewish communities of Judea and Samaria.

So I researched Congress's role with Israel and learned that it was mainly directed at defense-spending collaboration. The US government views Israel as its aircraft carrier in the Middle East—a stalwart ship surrounded by uncertain seas. Therefore, defending Israel is a chief US national security interest. Based on my research, I devised and scratched out on paper four potential objectives for leading advanced congressional education trips to Israel.

UNDER THE SMILE OF GOD

While I was researching, my organization was also building the National Center for Leadership in the city of Ariel. Mayor Ron Nachman received a call from Israel's defense minister, Ehud Barak, during the week of 9/9/09. The defense minister phoned to notify Ron that Jewish communities in Judea and Samaria would undergo a building freeze for the duration of the time that President Barack Obama was in office. This was a blow. Progress on the leadership center would come to a halt. The defense minister continued, "But I am going to exclusively give to you the licenses and permits needed to complete the National Center for Leadership in your city."

Ron thanked him and immediately called to give me the good and bad news. Ron always celebrated milestones with lots and lots of steak at a meal, and we had dinner that evening to celebrate the decision the defense minister had made concerning the National Leadership Center.

Steak was piled on my plate as if Ron and Dorit thought I was a ravenous lion. We ruminated over the outlandish miracle that all of Judea and Samaria had been placed under a building freeze except for the leadership center. "This leadership center must be under the smile of God," Ron said with a broad grin. "He will help us build this center for Israel."

I commented on the building freeze in Judea and Samaria, but I soon learned from Ron and his friends, who were mayors in the area, how destructive the freeze was for both the Palestinian and

Israeli economies. I thought more about how the US Congress needed to come and meet with leaders in Judea and Samaria to understand facts in context. While I still had not met a member of Congress, I was praying about bringing all of them to Israel.

In the summer of 2009, Tony Perkins, president of the Family Research Council in Washington, DC, came to JH Ranch with his daughter for a weeklong program. We had a conversation one day, and I asked him to have lunch with me. As we ate, I pulled out my scratch paper with the four objectives for an advanced education trip for Congress to Israel. As I explained what the Lord had shown me, he looked at me in disbelief. "You've got to be kidding," he said. "My last meeting in Washington on Friday was with US House Majority Leader Eric Cantor, who asked if I knew anyone who could help lead senior members of Congress on secondary trips to Israel." Tony then told me how surprised he was that Eric Cantor had asked him this, as Tony had never been to Israel, nor was Israel a part of the mission of the Family Research Council.

Two weeks later, I was sitting at the Capital Club in Washington, DC, with US House Majority Leader Eric Cantor, presenting my vision for advanced education trips for Congress to Israel. Eric Cantor was the highest-ranking Jewish leader in US history at the time, a gentle man who was well-respected politically on both sides of the aisle. He understood the growing need for advanced education trips to Israel. He knew we were building a leadership center in Samaria and that we had been involved there for a decade.

DOING WHAT ONE CAN

I laid out the objectives for an advanced tour, and Representative Cantor looked across the table at me and said, "This is outstanding. I will help you populate your tours." We began a partnership that day in order to set a new precedent in the US-Israel relationship.

A long season of prayer preceded our first tour in 2011. Certain things in life that we set out to do are easier to accomplish, but then in other situations, we surrender to impossible commands.

I would not be honest if I did not admit that I experienced a continuous inward battle of not wanting to move forward with the vision and not knowing how to create it. I was in the throes of building the National Leadership Center in Israel, working on my master's degree in theology, and Bruce and I had teenagers at home. Starting congressional tours to Israel seemed like a monumental task and was the last thing that seemed appropriate for me to do. As with the National Leadership Center, no financial resources existed for congressional tours, no organization formed to implement them, and no people assembled to support them.

I recalled the story of a sparrow who was lying in the street with its legs straight up in the air, sweating under its feathery arms. A warhorse walked up to the bird and asked, "What on earth are you doing?"

The sparrow replied, "I heard that the sky is falling, and I wanted to help."

The horse laughed a big, loud, sneering laugh, and said, "Do you really think you are going to hold back the sky with those scrawny little legs?"

The sparrow responded, "One does what one can."

I felt exactly like this sparrow. I would do what I could, which I did not think would be very much. God leads His talmidim into impossible assignments to break ground, to open up heaven's possibilities, and to bring justice where it is needed.

Jesus led His disciples into a relationship with Him that would impact the world of their day, even though their efforts may not have felt consequential to His disciples at the time. He made it clear to them from the get-go that in order to follow Him, they had to make unselfish decisions that would be incomprehensible to anyone seeking self-fulfillment. They would live sacrificial lives. Only in so doing would they expand their resources and do the things that Jesus had been doing.

THE SACRIFICIAL LIFE

God is attracted to courage and faith, even bird-size faith. He heard the prayers of the hairy prophet Elijah on Mt. Carmel when Israel had surrendered to Baal worship. In an unforgettable display of fireworks, God consumed the sacrifice, and 850 prophets of Baal and Asherah were wiped out in a single afternoon. Abraham obeyed God and prepared to offer his son on an altar, and God miraculously intervened and provided a ram to take his son's place. He was so pleased with Abraham's sacrifice that He made an eternal covenant with him and fulfilled His promise that he would be the father of many nations and the mediator of blessings to the world. We do our part, and God does His. The widow who dropped her two mites into the offering box was made famous by Jesus as having given more than anyone, and the unsuspecting young boy who shared his lunch watched it multiply to feed five thousand.

On a personal note, my life was so far outside the government sphere that I actually wondered if God cared about government. I felt like I was being sent into exile, government being the place God sends people who fall out of favor with Him. I felt like I had a plague. Senator James Lankford from Oklahoma, my wise friend who used to be a camp director before making a sharp turn to go into politics under God's leading, reminded me recently that thirty-six out of thirty-nine books of the Old Testament were written to, by, or about political leaders. One-third of New Testament stories involve Jesus' disciples interfacing with kings and rulers.

"From Moses to David and Solomon, who were leading the nation of Israel, to prophets like Daniel, Ezekiel, and the apostle Paul, who were assigned to kings," Senator Lankford said, "it is impossible to deny God's integral role in government. He cares about policy because it affects people very personally, and He cares about people."

Undoubtedly, governments all over the world represent the siren song of some of the angriest and most bitter of people, especially in the Middle East. However, God sends His talmidim into government time and again to live excellent lives in a secular world and to be uniquely set apart by Him to influence change. Senator Lankford asks, "Why are we so surprised that God leads His disciples into the darkest places on Earth to turn on the light and onto the most contested of battlefields to win battles?"

I knew that Judea and Samaria were uncharted territories, not to mention disputed, especially for world leaders, yet nevertheless it was home to where most of our Old Testament took place. Judea and Samaria is the land promised by the prophets to Israel as part of their final restoration. Ezekiel had foreseen Israel rebuilding their cities once again on the mountains of Judea and Samaria and taking possession of the land.[31]

PREPARING THE WAY

I knew we needed to prepare the way for the next stage of God's plan. We needed to educate Congress and unmask the false narratives that continued to undermine Israel's chances to keep those mountains under their control. Theologian and author Ray Anderson said, "Effective leadership is reading the signs of God's promises in the context of current events and translating those signs into goals. In this way, we prepare the way of the Lord."[32]

On that note, I formed the U.S. Israel Education Association and set out to create the tour of a lifetime for Congress, highlighting their important role in seeing the promises of God fulfilled

31 | Ezekiel 36

32 | Ray Anderson, *Minding God's Business* (Grand Rapids: Eerdmans Publishing, 1986), 65.

for Israel and the mutual benefits for the United States. We would meet with Israeli leaders and top experts and give them the best that was offered.

My staff and I facilitated our first organized congressional tour to Israel in November 2011, with five chairpersons and their spouses from the US House Armed Services Committee. I brought a team of my friends who are intercessors to pray ahead of us at different locations on the trip. This was a critical step. Prayer is like a battering ram slamming into a wall. God cooperates with the prayers of His talmidim to clear obstacles out of the way and prepare a road.

The day before we started the tour, I got cold feet and went to see Ron Nachman, who I considered to be not only my close friend but also a sage. We sat down in his living room, and he pulled out a cigar as I started to explain my concerns. He quietly listened, puffed some smoke, and asked, "Do you know the difference between a politician and a mountain?"

"No," I answered.

He said, "The closer you get to a politician, the smaller they become. The closer you get to a mountain, the bigger it becomes. You are the mountain. Just remember who you are. They will listen to you."

That was all I needed to hear. I went back to the hotel to prepare and then headed to the airport to pick up the delegation.

IRON DOME

Doug Lamborn, the congressman from Colorado, began to inquire on the first day about going to see Israel's Iron Dome, the new weapons defense system that intercepted rockets in midair as they were lobbed into Israel from Syria or the Gaza Strip. I looked at Congressman Lamborn like he had a screw loose. Then he asked me again the next day, and the day after that. I kept rolling my eyes, wondering how I would perform that feat.

The following day, we met with Prime Minister Netanyahu, and he gave a short briefing on the new Iron Dome Defense System as part of the US-Israel collaboration. At the end of the meeting, the prime minister directed a question to me. I dodged it and asked him if we could go see the Iron Dome. He looked at me and then whispered into the ear of one of his cabinet leaders. He folded his hands with resolve, nodded yes, and agreed to declassify Iron Dome by the following morning so the members could see it. We were amazed.

The following day, we became the first delegation of US leaders to see Israel's miracle-performing defense system. The members were flabbergasted by the technology. I recalled Isaiah's prophecy to Israel as our bus bumped along the dirt roads: *Foreigners will rebuild your walls, and their kings will serve you* (Isaiah 60:10). How fitting that the US (the foreigner) would take responsibility to help Israel create a wall of defense and share the financial load for Iron Dome, technology that would intercept hundreds and thousands of rockets over Israel in future years.

Upon their return to the United States, the members who were on our tour brought together the Foreign Affairs Committee and the Armed Services Committee and reviewed the importance of Israel's defense system as it relates to America's interests in the region. Two months later, this group of five congressmen, led by Congressman Lamborn, prepared legislation to triple the original budget for the missile defense system. It passed the House and Senate, and President Obama signed it.

We do not always have to know exactly what we are doing. We do have to show up and move forward, though, based upon what little we do know. Our initial congressional tour to Israel opened the playing field on Capitol Hill for our organization to facilitate many more briefings on Israel's multilayered defense weapons, which appropriated billions of dollars toward Israel's missile defense system.

The year after our initial congressional trip, Israel was put to the test by an egregious attack on its southern border when Hamas incited a war against Israel. Fortunately, Iron Dome installations had been placed in close proximity to all of the major cities and were 90 percent effective at intercepting and exploding the incoming rockets in midair, preventing Israel's cities from harm.

OPENING ROADS

On 11/11/11, my organization was at the close of our first congressional tour. We were in East Jerusalem, having traveled the winding roads of Judea and Samaria all day. The congressional leaders were moved to tears as they walked the biblical land they had always read about, visiting Shiloh, the childhood home of Samuel the prophet and the town where the ark of the covenant rested for 363 years. We drove down the Road of the Patriarchs, where Abraham had built his altars in Bethel and Hebron. Along the way, we stopped in Palestinian and Israeli communities—meeting mayors and other leaders and hearing from the people.

Unexpectedly, we pulled to the side of the road as one congressional member announced that it was 11:11 a.m. on 11/11/11. We decided to take a moment to pray that Judea and Samaria would remain one with Israel and to recognize Jerusalem as Israel's undivided capital. One by one, each member of Congress and their spouse prayed a pioneering-type of prayer—an audacious, hope-filled prayer about the future of Israel and peace with the neighboring nations.

That first congressional trip cleared the way for us to begin to educate and build, brick by brick, a new pathway for the US-Israel relationship. We began to see prejudices change in Congress toward Judea and Samaria, and legislation emerged in favor of Israel's strategic importance there, both for themselves and their vital role for the Palestinian people.

Five years after the road was opened for Congress to travel through Judea and Samaria, many unforeseeable breakthroughs occurred. It was like a dam breaking wide open, as things that had been on God's heart and our agenda for years began to take shape, such as the recognition of Jerusalem as Israel's capital, the move of the US embassy to Jerusalem, and significant changes to US State Department policy recognizing Israel's legitimacy and right to be in Judea and Samaria. Our organization worked closely with the US ambassador to Israel, David Friedman, to elevate joint business between Palestinians and Israelis. We also garnered bipartisan support for a piece of US legislation that passed in December 2020 and now formally requires US investment into Israeli-Palestinian business integration. We were able to see the US boycott removed from Judea and Samaria and to make a way for US-Israel collaboration in the areas of science, research, and development.

As I mentioned earlier, God's very first words to Abraham were *Lech, lecha*, or "Go, you!" That is, don't just stand there—*get going!* As God's first talmid, Abraham was given special promises that would determine the national and spiritual future of Israel. No one would set the framework for the future of Israel as he did. He was called to one simple task: listen and follow. Abraham cleared the way not just for himself and his immediate generation but for all talmidim after him who followed his lifestyle. Every believer who is a talmid today shares in Abraham's God-partnering call to listen and follow.

CHAPTER 7

TOGETHER

If you want to go fast, go alone.
If you want to go far, go together.

—African Proverb

I n the first century, the talmidim who met together in homes
every week were called the *ekklesia*, or "called-out ones." The
gatherings resembled a town hall meeting where members, who
took active roles in the community, met together. Citizens of all
shapes, sizes, and backgrounds attended these community meetings in a confluence of personalities. When one of them received
what they believed to be an assignment from God, the ekklesia
developed a strategy and shared the workload.

Based upon this New Testament paradigm, I am under
the strong impression that God does not entrust His most
important work to self-styled heroes or spiritual Miss Americas,

but to groups of talmidim who work closely together in small communities around a common vision. He trusts the talmidim's disciplined patterns of faith, prayer, and friendship because they have learned to walk together with agility and grace. They drop offenses between one another and seek one another's success. Jesus knew His talmidim before the foundations of the world. He knew they would need each other—not just for companionship, but as a band of brothers and sisters called into battle together. This is how God brings His kingdom to Earth through impossible situations. He trusts His talmidim with His work.

ENTRUSTED WITH THE WORK

It was a crisp November morning in Jerusalem, and I had been out for a fast walk in the Old City. As I arrived at the ninth floor of my hotel, I noticed two heavyset security guards standing down the hallway eating peanuts. The phone rang as I walked into my room. An associate had called to say that US Secretary of State John Kerry was staying in the room next to mine. "You've got to be kidding," was all I could say, and I hung up the phone.

I had no political qualms with John Kerry, but I was slightly bothered that he was in Jerusalem and I did not know the reason for his visit. My team and I had spent six months planning our trip down to the minute. It was 2013, and I had led numerous private congressional delegations to Israel. Because we were bringing the senior leaders of the US House, the last thing we needed was a curveball that would skew our meeting times with Israeli officials, which was highly likely with the last-minute arrival of a US administration official.

As I hurried to take a shower, the thought occurred to me that it might actually be divine timing that our delegation was in Jerusalem at the same time as the secretary of state.

Our delegation's meeting with Prime Minister Netanyahu had been changed to late afternoon. As we took our seats at the long conference table, the prime minister threw open the door, stormed into the room, and sat down at the table across from us with his staff and a few cabinet leaders. He was visibly shaken and disturbed. Forgetting his formal welcome, he launched into the meeting.

"Have you heard what just happened?"

Clueless, we all shook our heads no.

"Your secretary of state just informed me that the US, along with five permanent members of the UN Security Council, will begin work on a nuclear deal with Iran, our leading enemy. He told me that the worldwide sanctions on Iran, which have taken me ten years to establish, will be removed as Iran takes what they assure us will be trustworthy steps to stop nuclear weapon development. Secretary Kerry said that I must step aside so the UN Security Council members can negotiate this outrageous agreement."

He shook his head. "Today is the worst day in ten years for the nation of Israel—no, the worst day in two decades. And while you might not know it yet, this is also the worst day in decades or more for America. The terrorism that has plagued the Middle East is now headed to your shores."

He leaned forward. "Terrorists will now be coming to a theater near you. No longer will it be only Israel who lives under daily threat. This action will embolden Iran's delusion of a long-awaited Shia caliphate that will threaten the world. You will not see an end to Islamic terrorist attacks on American soil."

No one said a word. The prime minister slammed his fist into the table. "Do you understand what this means? The US is removing effective sanctions on Iran and awarding their nation with billions of dollars in trade from China and other nations under the delusion that they will honor their commitment to *not* build a nuclear bomb."

You could have heard a pin drop. The prime minister bowed his head in disbelief. He had been warning world leaders about the dangers presented by Iran and their terrorist proxies in the Middle East for more than ten years. On this day, his tone was radically different from any other day I had heard him speak. He sounded like a fiery prophet who had seen the future.

Steve Scalise, one of the leaders in our congressional delegation, quietly spoke. "This is hard to believe. We will meet to discuss what our steps will be as soon as we return to the US." Representatives Jim Jordan and Mike McIntyre echoed similar sentiments. The other congressional leaders sat in stunned silence.

The truth is that no one knew what to say to the prime minister.

Inwardly, my heart was breaking for him because he had fought so courageously to protect Israel—only to see more than a decade of investment slip from his hands.

A sharp pain penetrated my side and stayed with me the rest of the evening. Everyone in the room understood that we were privy to a decision that would impact the world. Certainly it had already impacted the leaders of Israel. The prime minister closed the meeting by saying, "Israel will do what it has to do, with or without the United States."

DIVINE TIMING

The members of Congress, like me, were stunned by the prime minister's distress. We returned to the hotel in silence. I slithered past the guards who were standing in my hall, and I entered my room with the pain still throbbing in my side. I thought about what it would be like to knock on John Kerry's door and ask him to please reconsider.

But of course, I couldn't—or could I? It seemed as if something very heroic needed to happen immediately, but I was helpless. I called my friends who were praying on the floor below me and gave them the news; then I laid in bed, stared at the ceiling, and prayed.

It had been my job to get the members of Congress to Israel. God had shown me the timeframe to bring them, and He knew that our Secretary of State would be in Jerusalem at the same time. He had orchestrated the timing of our meeting with Prime

Minister Netanyahu and his subsequent announcement to us. I went to sleep knowing that the news was now in the hands of Congress to decide what to do.

As if on cue, the members awoke the next morning challenged by Netanyahu's words, and they vowed to meet with their respective committees upon their return to the United States. Ted Poe, the chairman of the US House Foreign Affairs Committee, reported to his committee the prime minister's perspective of the newly conceived US plan to develop the Iranian nuclear deal.

Months later, the members from our tour opened the way for the Israeli prime minister to give his now renowned speech to the US House and Senate, during which Netanyahu reiterated the dire warnings he had stressed to congressional tour members previously in Jerusalem. The speech was heard around the world. He did not mince words as he explained the dangers of the Iran nuclear deal, called the Joint Comprehensive Plan of Action (JCPOA). To the prime minister's chagrin, President Obama moved ahead, in spite of his counsel, to enact the Iranian nuclear deal with the support of the UN Security Council and the approval of half of Congress.

Eerily, the words of the prime minister came true. Terrorists *did* arrive on US soil, and they *did* come to our theaters, nightclubs, and other venues throughout America. The spate of violence generated by the delusional ISIS terrorist proxy was not subverted until the Iranian nuclear treaty was overturned under the Trump administration, which led our US military to help destroy ISIS.

LOCKING ARMS

The insider truth is that amid disaster, God reserves a move on the chessboard for Himself and His talmidim that is far more strategic and multidimensional than our pea-sized brains can comprehend, or that we can accomplish on our own. He is also much less urgent about acting than we think He should be, like a slow-moving mechanic holding up the line at Express Oil Change. These things, of course, are a struggle for me.

The marvel of the world from the beginning of time is that God chooses to interact and partner with human beings. He doesn't need us. He chooses us. It is a crazy system, but He brings people together around a common vision and mission, and He compels them to stand between the problem on Earth and the reality of heaven. They band together and lock arms until there is a breakthrough. He trains His talmidim not to react in fear of pervading darkness, disappointment of others, or the seeming threat of circumstances. They refuse to jump to conclusions or take sides. They work in practical ways to facilitate God's plans and sack the enemy.

In an era of megachurches and constant online communication, it is even more vital for us to seek out a small community of talmidim who will invest in God's kingdom with us. Your vision may be a new business venture, a mission that needs your gifts, a government policy that needs to be changed, or an outreach that needs your time and energy. We need to find our vision and our tribe.

I knew that our organization—along with the members of Congress who were in the meeting with the prime minister and my friends who were praying at the hotel—would make an important contribution to the outcome of the predicament between the United States and Israel. We were eyewitnesses to the sticky, complicated problem, so we set up a weekly meeting to pray into the dilemma as if we had been given a corner of Israel's wall to defend. Everyone took the responsibility seriously, and we recruited others to join. We asked God for His view of the situation, we received His promises, and we invoked His mercy.

On the practical side, our organization arranged for experts to educate US leaders on Capitol Hill so that Congress could further investigate the Iranian nuclear deal (JCPOA) in view of America's national security interests. Everyone cooperated and did their part.

PARTNERS IN PROPHECY

Two years after the disturbing meeting with Prime Minister Netanyahu, I was back in Jerusalem in another meeting with him and members of Congress. Once again, his message was about Iran and the need to reinstate sanctions on their economy.

After an hour, the prime minister asked me a question in front of everyone, which prompted me to tell him about the biblical prophecies in Isaiah concerning the kings who would play a role in the building of modern Israel. I talked about Isaiah 60:10–12:

> *Foreigners will rebuild your walls, and their kings*
> *will serve you. . . . Your gates will always stand open,*

they will never be shut, day or night, so that peo-
ple may bring you the wealth of the nations—their
kings led in triumphal procession. For the nation or
kingdom that will not serve you will perish; it will
be utterly ruined.

I highlighted for him that according to biblical prophecies, a forthcoming group of international rulers would serve Israel, seek alliances, and strengthen the nation. The prime minister looked at me intently over the top of his glasses. He closed the meeting, said farewell to our congressional delegation, and asked if I would meet him in his office. I got up and followed him.

When we got to his office, he motioned for me to sit down. He told me he had been studying the book of Isaiah with his son and thought it was ironic that he had just read the exact verses I had quoted in the meeting. "Why do you know those verses by memory?" he asked.

I told him I had been teaching Congress on this subject for several years in order to help them understand their role as US leaders with Israel.

Then he asked me an audacious, searching question: "Do you think the verses you quoted are for now or for a future time?"

I awkwardly laughed and told him that maybe he should think about asking God instead of me. But then I eked out my interpretation. I told him that I thought he should expect a number of nations to pursue alliances with Israel in order to benefit from

Israel's technology, industry, intelligence, and military strength. Isaiah had foreseen that kings from other nations would serve Israel and invest there during the time of her restoration and rebuilding.

I also told the prime minister that this influx of leaders from other nations pursuing Israel could happen at any time. I encouraged him not to fear any US leader who did not espouse his warnings about Iran because God would fill in the gaps, including other heads of state who would influence America. He concurred that this scenario was probable, and he thanked me.

Then the prime minister opened his desk drawer and pulled out an ancient coin that had been discovered under the Temple Mount. The name "Netanyahu," a ruler of Israel from ancient times, was inscribed on it in Hebrew. He had shown it to me once before, but this time he asked me what I thought about it. I told him that it seemed like a personal sign from God that he had been chosen to lead Israel at this specific time and that he should expect God to be present with him for anything he needs. I told him about the significant number of people who pray for him and for Israel every day. We ended our conversation, he thanked me, and I went out into the night to meet our delegation. I sensed that the daunting concern about Iran in the prime minister's mind would take an extraordinary turn. It did.

God played His sovereign hand, and important factors suddenly shifted, but not until years later—in 2020. A universe-sized twist of fate was underway, led by US President Trump, the UAE,

Bahrain, and other Middle East regional actors who had grown
fearful of the possibility of Iran as a future nuclear power. These
nations turned to none other than Israel for safe harbor as *the* military
superpower of the Middle East. Five years after the Iranian
nuclear deal was initiated, Arab nations, one by one, dropped their
long-standing embargo against Israel and set in motion treaties for
trade, military intelligence, and diplomatic relations.

As I stood on the lawn of the White House in August 2020
for the signing of the Abraham Accords between Israel, the US,
Bahrain, and the UAE, I knew with certainty that Israel's standing
in the world had changed overnight. They would be stronger.
None of the Arab gulf states could afford to be unprepared for a
nuclear Iran. The Arab nations needed Israel, and Israel needed
the Arab nations, and they will continue to need each other in the
face of the Iranian threat.

I walked back to my hotel on this momentous day, mindful
that Isaiah's prophecies about nations that would serve and benefit
from Israel were coming to the fore in my lifetime. While Iran
remains a serious threat and the future is unknown, a significant
cosmic shift occurred under God's almighty hand. Many people
had worked together fulfilling elements of His plan over a period
of years to see the monumental milestone of the Abraham Accords
finally realized under the Trump administration.

Most humbling of all is to comprehend that our pit crew of
friends stood together, sharing audacious prayers, enduring the

intensity of the journey, contributing to the collaborations, and daring to believe that God would do the impossible—partner with us to bring the kingdom of heaven to Earth.

CHAPTER 8

FINDING HOME

Where I am most inwardly myself,
there You are, O God, far more than I.

—St. Augustine

As children and young adults, we share a wild anticipation that we will live out our dreams, even if our dreams happen to be very shallow (I think my dreams must have been). People come along and affirm our romantic ideals, and before long we set sail toward our enchanted rainbow.

But more than the fulfillment of our dreams, personal relationships shape much of who we become. John Macmurray, the twentieth-century Scottish philosopher, explains that we are who we are only in relation to others. Essentially, he says that we are all like lumps of Play-Doh that only take on a unique shape through our active connection with others. Meaningful relationships, including our dynamic relationship with God, give us our individual uniqueness and bring us into full maturity as persons. God's aim in giving us specific, worthwhile connections is to help shape our identity.

CONSEQUENTIAL RELATIONSHIPS

As an example, our God-given parental role is to lay the significant foundation of our children's early lives and to be the primary platform for their personal development. Without a healthy, positive family life, we are left with deep needs for God to fill—and some of these holes can feel like caverns.

Too often, the most terrible situations that people barely survive happen within their families. This is sad but true. One of the primary ways that God stitches people's lives back together is through meaningful, safe friendships where we can recover from pain and become our unique selves, living full, free lives. It is astonishing to watch someone who has been broken by abuse acknowledge that they have been set free from toxic dependency, crippling guilt, and obsession, and that they have been given the grace to truly forgive the person or people who harmed them—as well as themselves. Only God can do that kind of work in us, and it requires the support of loving friends. When we search for answers to life's toughest questions, God often sends us consequential relationships instead, which is far better.

A COMPASSIONATE FATHER

My dad brought a lot of humor to our home. Some fathers take their children's fears away, and others produce and reinforce fear. My father was the former. He had a collection of outrageous costumes and wigs that filled our attic and would be employed at any given moment. My dad was the Patch Adams of our social circle. He never showed up to a party or an event without a carefully selected costume and a range of entertaining songs, jokes, and impersonations.

If you were ever around my dad and you had a distinctive feature of any kind, he would imitate you. He couldn't resist doing this. My mom, sisters, and I lived with an impersonator, and we laughed hard a lot of the time. When I was a child and would spend the night at friends' houses, I always wondered why their dads acted so seriously.

Everyone wanted to be around my father. He drove a huge red Buick convertible, and my sisters and I would pile in with friends and sit on the edge of the back seat with the wind blowing in our hair as we loudly sang our favorite songs by Helen Reddy, Eric Clapton, the Rolling Stones, and Michael Jackson. During my senior year of high school, my friends and I taped all of the names of our classmates on the hood and back of the car so it could be featured as the senior class car in the school parade. I honestly thought this was a brilliant idea, and my heart swelled with pride.

Unfortunately, my friends and I were far more motivated to tape the names onto the car in anticipation of the parade rather than to remove them afterward. The tape baked in the sun over the weekend, and the names of my senior class melted into the paint in an embarrassing disaster.

Even with such a huge mess and the need for an expensive paint job, it never occurred to me to fear my dad's response. I never received a lecture on responsibility like most teenagers would have gotten. Never once in my life did my dad say anything like, "I've had it this time. You've gone too far, and you are grounded for six weeks. Now go live in the garage." My dad was generous and forgiving, and he always invited me back. All I needed to do was to tell him I was sorry for my irresponsibility, and he took me at my word. His consistent, gentle responses reinforced an attitude of respect in my sisters and me and made us want to please him.

Dad quietly got the car repainted without shaming me. This may sound scandalous and lacking in parental common sense, but I am convinced this is what God's love looks like.

Because of his compassionate candor, my dad was often at odds as an attorney in an aggressive, cutthroat legal world. He made friends outside of his social circle just as much as inside his social circle, and he often befriended the man in the ditch, the person who was bankrupt, the client who could not pay his fee, and those who were poor and needed to be defended the most. He cared about people who were in unfortunate situations, and he eagerly worked for them.

LOVE THAT ERASES FEAR

My father's steadiness, laughter, and belief in me gave me freedom to envision a life of unfettered love in the nation of Israel—far outside my cultural setting and social circle. In removing my fears, my dad removed my limitations, both emotionally and mentally. Leading congressional tours and facilitating a new level in the US-Israel relationship had been nowhere in my repertoire of dreams. However, when the Lord guided me "off the map" with love for Israel, my mother and father unswervingly believed that I could do anything with God's help, even without a formal political education.

My dad was too lighthearted to ever guide me in a serious way. I had a real need for strong, unintimidating leadership, so God brought other people into my life to fill that role. I believe this is how He works. No human being is a complete package of perfectly blended virtues and character qualities. The sooner we understand this, the sooner we can release our unrealistic expectations about how we think people should fulfill our needs. We can let go of what we think they should do for us and embrace a larger community of friends as we look to God to fill the holes in our lives.

Our relationships with others—whether we are close or at a distance—have a profound impact on who we become. A disciple needs to embrace relationships and read books about others that not only inspire growth but also, as Franz Kafka wrote to Oscar Plook in 1904, "bite us and sting us." We need friends and mentors who become the "axe for the frozen sea within us."[33]

33 | Alberto Manguel, A History of Reading, Toronto: Vintage Books, 1998, pg 93

HOLY MENTORS

My mentor and spiritual father for the last twenty years, Dr. James Houston, played this role in my life. He filled holes my father could not fill. He did this by asking real and often painful, upsetting questions that went beyond the surface of my charming Southern behavior, removing obstacles that prevented me from getting to the heart of the matter. I deeply resented this at times. *Why can't you just see the good in me?* I have sometimes thought to myself.

Dr. Houston, with all of his tenderness, loved me deeply enough to prepare me for the winding road of a disciple and a life of courageous decision-making. I will never forget when I met him. It was my first day of theology school, and he was the visiting professor from Regent College in Vancouver, which he founded. I was astounded by his teaching. After the class ended, I waited for everyone to leave. I turned off the lights and laid on the floor to make a strong point with God that I wanted this man to become my spiritual father, one of my guides and friends.

Dr. Houston took me out to lunch one day, as he did with every person in our class, reflecting his policy of becoming personally acquainted with each of his students. At the age of eighty-three, he looked me in the eyes and read my soul. The experience was both scary and holy. I immediately knew that what he was telling me about my future, the personal warnings he was giving me, and the care in his eyes were from God. I knew I could trust him.

Dr. Houston was (and still is) a holy man, one who forfeited his personal ambitions and left the esteemed Oxford University, where he was a professor and friend of C. S. Lewis, to pioneer a new school in a foreign country for the purpose of preparing disciples. I must admit that I chased Dr. Houston like he was Elvis. My pursuit was embarrassingly uncomfortable because I pressed in to try to capture some of his time, and I think I was annoying. Truthfully, I gratefully took any time he would give me, and only after a certain amount of time did he begin to take me seriously. I am glad I pursued him relentlessly because our relationship became one of the weightiest I have ever experienced.

Dr. Houston has mentored me now for almost twenty years. He has not only been my spiritual guide, who has lived ahead of me under the yoke of Jesus, but he has also been a source of clarification to me as I have addressed top leaders of the nation of Israel concerning the problem of untenable secularism, which is the absence of God in society.

Dr. Houston helped me gather my words time and again when I repeatedly asked the leaders of Israel's Ministry of Education, "Did God bring you back to Israel to give you safety and autonomy, or were His purposes greater? Was it not His favor toward you that brought you from the four corners of the earth in order to give you identity, to show you who you really are? How, then, can Israel live into the promise of being a 'light to nations' while retaining an abstract view of God and never becoming personal with Him?

And finally, why would a new generation want to stay in Israel, the most contested place on Earth, if they are not motivated to be there by the virtues of their biblical heritage and identity?"

Over the years, these conversations resulted in biblical heritage content being incorporated into Israel's high schools, as well as being given the platform to build Israel's National Leadership Center as the medium for influencing a nation to know God in a personal way.

Dr. Houston is now ninety-eight years old, and we continue to enjoy a close friendship. He still takes walks with his students, doing all he can to guide them in their spiritual journeys. He recently wrote in his memoir, "When impartation is more intimate, it demands a personal experience with God that is more radical and is experienced more deeply in one's innermost being."[34]

My dad and Dr. Houston played wildly different roles in my life. Both were fathers to me. My dad was generous and kindhearted, and Dr. Houston was a refining tool. Both men helped me discover the main point of life—that I am deeply and irreversibly loved by God and have the courage to obey the Lord and make brave decisions. Regardless of our family background, God gives us meaningful relationships to reveal His love to us and help us become who He created us to be.

---

34 | James Houston, *Joyful Exiles: Life in Christ on the Dangerous Edge of Things* (Downers Grove, IL: InterVarsity Press, 2006), 111–112.

VISION FOR WHO WE ARE BECOMING

Peter, Jesus' disciple, also went through a rigorous and challenging process with the person he admired most, and it changed everything for him. As a loyal talmid of Jesus, Peter was passionate. Over a three-year period, he made impressive announcements about his love and commitment to Jesus. Jesus saw who he was becoming, and He changed his name from Simon to Peter, meaning "rock."

But before Peter was a rock, he was a sandpile. Jesus saw that Peter's fragile image of himself, his superior attitude over others, and his belief that he could succeed by himself would soon crumble. Jesus gave Peter advance notice that he would deny Him, the very thing Peter swore he wouldn't do. I don't know about you, but I prefer to make my mistakes in private with low visibility. Can you imagine the worst mistake of your life being told from generation to generation to the whole world?

A climactic turn of events culminated on the shores of the Sea of Galilee. The redemption of the entire world had occurred just days before, and the victory had been won; yet to Jesus' straggling talmidim who were waiting in the Galilee, power and victory had not become real.

The disciples pushed their boat into the water and bobbed up and down all night without catching a single fish. At dawn, a voice called from across the lake: "Friends, haven't you any fish yet?"

"No," was the reply.

In a matter of moments, 153 glimmering fish darted across the lake and leapt into the disciples' nets.[35] As fishing stories go, none would ever be as great as this one. The number 153 in Hebrew means *Ani Elohim*, "I am Lord over." In the most real sense, Jesus was announcing from the shore, "I am Lord over your future, your identity, and your destiny." In other words, "I am about to heal your deep disappointment and take you forward from here."

Peter realized that Jesus was calling from the shore. Amid the fish miracle, Peter threw on his robe and dove into the water for his famous swim to shore. At his deepest level of vulnerability, Peter realized that he had to be deeply honest in order to receive acceptance from the One he had been striving so hard to please. He saw no use of hiding in the hull of the boat with his unbearable failure and disappointment. In his swim to Jesus, he made the all-important decision to forego self-hatred, insecurity, and his diseased emotions about himself.

The swim was not a small thing. It was everything. Nothing in Peter's life could have moved forward without this step of courage. In being received as he was rather than as he should be, everything about Peter would change. A new person would emerge through his encounter with Jesus. The ordeal would restore him to himself.

It takes guts to swim to shore with your dismal failures and death of vision about who you think you are. In 2019 I was leading a US congressional tour to Israel when my good friend Congresswoman Cathy Rodgers and I decided to swim to shore. Cathy carries a heavy load of leadership on Capitol Hill and lives

35 | John 21:1–14

in an environment of ruthless battles. We became friends on a previous trip to Israel, but on this trip we shared a milestone moment.

Cathy and I walked down the shoreline and talked vulnerably about the challenges of leadership and about our need for rest, approval, and significance. It was an impromptu moment, but we decided to mark an experience together whereby we deeply understood that we were forgiven as well as approved of by God. We walked into the Sea of Galilee fully clothed and with our sandals on, and we swam about fifty yards out in the lake. We then treaded water and prayed together, turned our shaky selves over to Jesus, and swam back as His renewed daughters.

I will never forget that experience as long as I live. My personal life, which has been marked at times with depression, anxiety, and serious disappointment with myself, required infusions of courage to turn my trembling self over to the One who loves me with my weaknesses, as well as to friends who care deeply.

UNVARNISHED TRANSPARENCY
AND IRREVERSIBLE CONFIDENCE

There is always mental justification for staying depressed and angry, but breakthrough cannot happen amid our resistance. It is not popular to say it today, but *what is hidden cannot be healed.* We can construct an impressive identity, a vision of grandeur about ourselves, and the world around us can buy into it—only to realize that inside, we are as fragile as a house of cards. Relief comes from unvarnished honesty about ourselves as we hand our disappointments over to Jesus. Where we are most honest with God and ourselves, we find Him most intimately to be our Father and healer. Augustine said, "Where I am most deeply myself, there You are, O God, far more than I."

Jesus had one aim in serving a lakeside breakfast that morning: He wanted His disciples, especially Peter, to become irreversibly confident of His love. The meal on the seashore with Jesus would heal them, reinstate them, and define who they were. It was a meal of acceptance. The disciples had experienced their own failures, but now the best of possibilities could happen, for it would be God's love, and His love alone, on which the gospel of the kingdom would go to the world through His talmidim.

His love for them could not be a hazy concept. They had to go through a real test, and His love had to be put on trial amid their abysmal failures. The success of the gospel would not and could not depend on their fickle natures and fragile identities but rather upon their confident belief that Jesus fully accepted them. How else could broken earthen vessels become channels of living water?

SEEING DIFFERENTLY

This transformative experience in Galilee was deeply personal. The disciples came to understand themselves differently. Isn't there a paradox here that the things that cause us the greatest personal suffering are the springboards that free us from ourselves in ways that we would never have imagined?

Amid the disciples' feelings of disorientation and homeless-ness, they understood with new clarity and resolve that Jesus was holding all things together. Peter's intimate confrontation with Jesus enabled him to give the rest of his life in sacrificial love for others, just as Jesus had so personally done for him. Peter was given a new identity and came into full maturity as a person, not because his dreams were fulfilled, but because Jesus took him beyond what he thought he could ever be and called him to a life beyond comprehension.[36]

Jesus fills the cavernous holes of our unsteady lives as He speaks to us about who we are to Him. He gives us an identity unlike any earthly father can give, and He puts His trust in us, knowing full well our soul-shattering failures and weaknesses. He uses meaningful and sometimes unlikely relationships to reveal His multifaceted love and to help us become who we are in Him. In so doing, His love empowers us to live as talmidim, uniquely positioned and poised to shape the world around us.

36 | John 6:44, 63, 65; 17:2

CHAPTER 9

SOLITUDE, SILENCE, LISTENING

And in the morning, rising up,
a great while before day, he went out,
and departed into a solitary place...

—Mark 1:35 KJV

W e live one day at a time, and some of us are aware that
life will be over too soon. Click. The watch stops. Time
for blood pressure pills and rapid wrinkle remover. That will be
$500, please. Recently, I have been putting thick potions on my
fine lines and wrinkles, trying to smooth them out. As I look in
the mirror, I am reminded that it was a good thing that I woke up
one morning, earlier in my life, desperate to not waste any more
time obsessing and striving for what is meaningless. We all have

a human need to know that we have lived a life of meaning from the true essence of who we are.

THE NECESSITY OF SOLITUDE

We are not superstars. We need rest and solitude—every year, each week, and some part of every day. If we were convinced that the true essence of our being and our far-reaching accomplishments were contingent on our time of solitude with God, wouldn't even the mother of small children and the busy executive find a way to stop everything and make time to listen to Him? However, many of us see solitude as a luxury that is out of reach. Is it? Is solitude a luxury or a necessity? Why is it such a revolutionary thought that the most important time we spend in life is when we are alone with God?

When we connect with God, we connect better to ourselves and to others. The inverse is also true. When we are strangers to Him, we are strangers to ourselves and to others.

The core of who I am is best refreshed and rediscovered in solitude. Although it was often inconvenient, I scheduled short, personal retreats away from home when our children were young. When I stepped out, Bruce stepped in to help with the kids. We supported each other's solitude in this way. Quiet time alone, contemplation, prayer, music, reading, or small creative projects helped me renew my spirit and center myself. The effort took planning, but the time I invested paid off in physical and spiritual

renewal. I get it—all of us have vastly different living situations. I have friends who are single moms who would grab "mini retreats" in the bathroom for ten minutes—but you get my point.

My mother imparted to me the practice of Scripture reading and reflection and it was one of the most important gifts I have ever received. When I was in the fifth grade, she gave each of my sisters and me a set of junior devotionals and a small spiral notebook. I started a ritual of reading and writing every day. Every morning, my mother could be found reading her Bible. This was her time alone to pray and be with God. Consequently, the morning became a window of solitude for my sisters and me as well. As a result, disciplined Scripture reading and meditation hold deep significance for me.

Developing a ritual of solitude is like making a steady deposit into your bank account, and wouldn't it be really nice if you could actually do that? After significant daily installments over a period of time, think how rich you would become if you did not overspend. Solitude creates a pathway to the future, keeping us on track to be the person we want to be instead of devolving into a lazy, crying, wimpy alternative of ourselves.

THE VALUE OF LIMITATIONS

If we took our humanity seriously and did not over-spiritualize our efforts, we would recognize the value of human limitations. We would stop trying to do too much and to be too much. I have found that exhaustion is the dark ghost of our generation. Is it not one of the leading reasons spiritual leaders fall into unintended double lifestyles of sexual impurity that they cannot renounce? Is exhaustion not a source of addiction, mistaken desires, greed, and misguided passion?

Exhaustion creeps up on us when we exceed the limitations of our humanity. We tell ourselves that we have a grip on our schedules and our strength and fortitude, so we drive ourselves harder and push and overplay our hand. Granted, everyone has to respond to certain things that are beyond their control, but too often we sacrifice and give until our inner springs become dry and cracked—and still we continue to justify our choices over and over again. Many people regard exhaustion as a virtue that accompanies a sacrificial life.

Western culture honors exhausted people who do superhuman amounts of work while leaving mangled people in their wake. We think exhaustion is the lesser thing on the scale of negative things you could do to yourself. We think we will recuperate, but the truth is that after months and years of pushing ourselves beyond our limits, we do not fully recuperate from exhaustion. Draining ourselves dry impacts our will, as well as our personality and choices. Ultimately, it degrades our character and slowly bankrupts our human desires. As we become vulnerable to temptation, we cross lines that we never would have crossed if exhaustion and its effects had not taken hold of us.

TERRORIST IN THE FRONT YARD

In 2014, I was diagnosed with breast cancer and had to have surgery. The news was shocking, potent, and traumatizing, like a well-organized terrorist attack in my front yard. Bruce and I had been under a strain in our marriage due to unresolved extenuating family issues. I was also in charge of two growing organizations and did not have enough help. I was driving hard and fast, but with the doctor's report, my life came to a complete standstill.

I laid in bed and stared at the ceiling, utterly relieved to be resting and not working. I desperately needed to stop and rebuild. From my diet to needed exercise, to getting our marital issue resolved once and for all, to my urgent need for more employees, I saw my glaring limitations and my need for help in every area of life. I was only in my forties. How could I be facing a life-threatening disease?

My healing process took time. I needed six months off and an about-face in how I approached work and processed my thoughts and emotions. My health crisis became a turning point in my marriage, as it forced Bruce and me to address a longstanding issue: we had to become agents of healing to one another. How surreal that we were shaping the world with our work but at the same time were sources of hurt to each other in our marriage.

THE GIFT OF GUIDELINES

During this season of change, Bruce and I made tough decisions together that impacted both us and people around us. However, our decisions were critical to our health and healing, as well as to the well-being of everyone under our care. During this important period of time, my life was strengthened and I could see more clearly what I needed to do and what I needed to delegate to others. I realized I could no longer give myself away in a manner that threw me off balance, so I created permanent guidelines for the future. These guidelines were both a gift and an act of responsibility to those I love.

More than anything, though, I needed a renewed mind that was flowing with God. I wanted to have wise and powerful actions as opposed to an unrenewed mind that leads to unwise and uncalculated actions. Solitude paves the way for us to discern God's will and follow His voice.

As God's talmidim, we need time to cultivate the hidden depths of a centered life. We need time to learn to distinguish between God's voice and the world, and between the Holy Spirit and our own spirit. A talmid of Jesus has to create a personal environment that is conducive to listening. Lesser things have to be cleared away to make room for the sacrosanct. This takes discipline, ritual, and passion for Him—just Him.

As prominent and hallowed as social media is, one would think that people would be more connected than ever, like at the peace-loving, hippie music festivals of the sixties, but the opposite is true. Psychologists report that people are lonelier and more alienated than ever, that relationships are distant and ambiguous, and that people are less focused than they used to be. Not only do people strive to find their identity in the context of today's latest trend, but they also spend countless hours scouring their feed with the overwhelming sensation of FOMO—or Fear of Missing Out, as I am told by the younger people. It is no wonder that we have to work harder than preceding generations to create our own "wilderness experiences" in order to find God for ourselves.

To be a true disciple with a strong identity, we need to be able to walk very personally with Jesus without a handrail of spiritual input from others. We have to pull away from our therapeutic spiritual culture and technology to create a direct route to God. This requires radical resolve and focus.

In the stark simplicity of a vast wilderness, Jesus listened to His Father's voice and absorbed His words for more than forty days. He emerged from the desert in the power of the Holy Spirit. We marvel at this and wonder how we could have defining experiences like His, especially since we cannot abandon our work responsibilities and families and take forty days off or live like a hermit or a desert father. How do we align our lives for a more ardent union with Him?

A thirst for oneness with Jesus is the primary motivation of a talmid. Individual sacrifices are needed to create a lifestyle of regular solitude. Sacrifices are also needed inside of marriages in an effort to allow each other time for solitude.

THE PRIORITY OF SOLITUDE

I will never forget my first twenty-four-hour solo in the wilderness at the age of seventeen in the mountains above JH Ranch. A group of persistent ants were building a castle with a moat nearby. Although it could have been my imagination, I think there was a twelve-foot bear circling the perimeter of my quiet space, licking his chops while waiting for me to open my canned beef stew. Besides that, everything went mostly as planned.

I experienced God in as many ways as I possibly could have in that first solo time. My teenage concerns were healed by staring at the beauty of the crystal blue lake. I was quieted by the dead silence of the wilderness, and I could hear His impressions about both simple and complex things. I wrote down everything I thought He was saying. The experience was so powerful that from that point on, I never stopped scheduling times of complete silence and solitude.

The word "obedient" comes from the Latin word *audire*, which means "listening." To move from a distracted life to an obedient one, from a life filled with noisy worry to a life where we experience a free inner space where we can listen, is to experience life as He intended it.[37] Jesus was always *listening* to His Father, which means He was always *obeying* His Father. Listening requires us to align our hearts to be led rather than to follow our own lead. We don't discover God through analysis but through surrender. Our surrender is what attracts His voice. He seems to conceal His truth and leading so that only the hungry find Him.

37 | Henri J. M. Nouwen, *Making All Things New* (New York: HarperCollins Publishers, 1981), 82.

Comprehension is not always evidence that we have heard from Him because God is beyond our reach and understanding. Sometimes we are unaware that He is speaking to us, but some brilliant idea pops into our head and becomes a contribution inside of our workplace, or we have a sudden realization about how to correct a complex problem. God speaks uniquely to each of His disciples. One thing we know is that we all are expected to hear from God and to discover our own unique way of listening to Him.

Developing a regular pattern helps. There are ways to increase our ability to recognize His voice. I discovered that listening to the Holy Spirit can become a regular exercise. To have a regular pattern—a time and an uncluttered place that is free from work, distraction, and technology—is to create a pathway for hearing Him. It is sort of like looking into the shallow water of a birdbath. We see our reflection to the degree that the sunlight enables us. A particle or a leaf can fall into the water and shatter the image we see. Having a specific time, place, and plan clears the way for less interruption.

I have noticed that God speaks to the people who have pen and paper handy. This might sound pedantic, but think about it. Jeremiah had a scroll and probably some ink and some sort of feathery quill. Ezekiel had papyrus and a way to write down what he was hearing. Paul wrote down what he heard from prison. God trusted His talmidim to write down what they were hearing so they could relay or do what He was saying. It could have been easy for Ezekiel to think, *I don't need to write down this vision of Israel returning from captivity. Somebody else will do it.* However, God didn't have anyone else to do what He was asking Ezekiel to do.

Our daily exercise with Him should involve reading small portions of Scripture each day and listening to what He says as it relates to us personally—either a circumstance in our life or someone we know. We can specifically ask the Holy Spirit to counsel us as we read the Word and help us apply what we are reading.[38] We can pray in response to Psalm 32:8, *Thank You, Holy Spirit, that You will instruct me and teach me in the way I should go. You will counsel me with Your eye upon me.*

In an exercise of sitting quietly to listen, the aim is not to try to study the Bible for comprehension or to find truth but to seek His counsel for our personal life in *real* time. It is a good practice to write down the verses you are reading. You can ask a simple question like, "How do You want me to apply this to my life?" which may be obvious, or you could ask, "Is there anything I need to do about this today?" This seems so basic, but I believe that when we consistently lean into an exercise like this one, God increases our ability to hear His voice. He enlarges our capacity for more responsibility and assignments from Him because He can trust that we will listen and follow.

Our time of solitude should naturally overflow into our sphere of influence and should impact those around us. Cultivating a listening ear is a tangible act of true surrender to God's will above our

38 | Isaiah 50:4

own. Listening is the platform for our obedience and oneness with Him, and it is one of the central characteristics of living under an easy yoke as a talmid of Jesus.

SOLITUDE AND TRANSFORMATION

When I think of solitude, my mind wanders to the mountains of northern California. JH Ranch is a breathtaking place. When you drive across the wooden bridge, you notice a sprawling open field of daisies bumping up against the white-capped purple Salmon Mountains. In the middle of the field stands a high-peaked white festive tent where parents and their children come in the evening to talk about life's most important questions. JH Ranch is where guests take a break from a competitive world that demands their attention and where people meet God face to face and are healed.

God is uniquely present at JH Ranch in the same way that people feel Him in Jerusalem. I don't have an explanation for this, except that we really wanted Him at JH—to encounter people, to transform their marriages and relationships, and to set them free from addictions and obsessions. Bruce's parents, Gene and Joy Johnston, purchased JH Ranch in 1979 with the vision to create a retreat for people to find God. Little did they know that their vision would not be contained to JH Ranch but would stretch across the country and around the globe for the healing of families.

Some guests would say they stumble upon grace at JH Ranch— grace they didn't have fifteen minutes before they arrived. They are suddenly able to forgive some pretty horrible people and to let go of bitterness. I am sure God has a lot of special places like JH Ranch in the world where He routinely heals people.

Early in our adventure, Bruce and I faced the stark reality of how far JH Ranch was from civilization—forty-five minutes from the closest Walmart and an hour and a half from anything culturally soothing. Why wouldn't people just decide to go to Camp Tomahawk down the street from where they lived? Why fly across the country—or in many cases, internationally—to northern California, and then drive five hours to JH Ranch? Why would anyone do that unless they had a sense of certainty that they would meet God on the mountain and hear Him speak—or that He would fix their relationship with their teenager, parent, or spouse—or that they would gain something that they couldn't get anywhere else?

Bruce and I started an annual ritual in which we walked around the property and prayed over it to make sure God knew we really wanted Him there. I know God is everywhere, even at Costco and Publix, but we wanted His presence in a different way at JH Ranch, with His breath on our faces. We built small altars and took communion and repeated our ritual of prayer, walking the property year after year. We felt like our job was to host people in such a way that they could meet God there.

WHEN GOD SPEAKS

Because of this, it was not surprising when Eran Glazer, a Jewish education leader from Tel Aviv, arrived with his delegation at

JH Ranch without a spiritual life and then began to hear God. He was under the impression that JH Ranch was near New York City and that his days would be spent learning; then he would head into Times Square for some big nightlife. Needless to say, he was a bubble off—maybe several bubbles!

When he climbed the Leap of Faith, a freestanding pole with a trapeze seven feet up and seven feet out from the pole, I had sized him up physically and was not expecting him to be able to jump from the pole and catch the trapeze—but he did. After he repelled back to the ground, he walked to lunch with me and told me that he had heard an audible voice speak to him in Hebrew from the pine trees, and he asked me if I thought it was God speaking to him.

I looked at him inquisitively and asked him what he had heard. "I heard I am going to bring a child into the world," he answered.

I asked him if those words meant something to him, and he nodded. "Yes, my wife and I are trying to have another baby, and I lead the largest youth movements in the State of Israel, so children mean a lot to me."

I told him that it sure did sound like God but that he should inquire further. After lunch, we walked to our bookstore, and I got Eran a journal, a pen, and a Hebrew Bible with the book of Psalms. I quickly explained that God speaks to people who are seeking Him. I pointed to the mountains just above us and sent him on a hike to find God for himself—with no devotional books, no prayer, and no further guidance from me. "Just go," I said. "God will speak to you. Write down what you hear."

Eran believed it, and it happened. He came down the mountain several hours later with a notebook filled with written pages of what he had heard from God. There is no need to tell you that this experience changed his life forever. There had been no coaching and no interference. God met Eran personally. God revealed to him that his life's purpose was to love and serve Him and others. Not too long after that, he quit his prestigious job overseeing the youth movements of Israel in order to help me pioneer the National Leadership Center that we built on the hills of Samaria. He became the leader and brought tens of thousands of youth into a personal walk with God.

We can have as much of God as we want, but how willing are we to get alone and practice a rhythm of solitude in order to have Him be dynamically present in our lives?

Eran left JH Ranch having adopted the song "Open the Eyes of My Heart." Indeed, Eran truly wanted to see God. He made that song the ringtone on his phone, and he listened to it every day. He sang it like a prayer so many times that the song became his reality. He began to see into the spiritual realm and to hear clearly from God. As a result, he did exactly what Bruce and I did at JH Ranch: he walked the property of the National Leadership Center in Israel in order to establish the property as a place of *emunah*, or faith—a place where God heals people and speaks to them personally. More than eighty-five thousand students have gone through Israel's National Center for Leadership since Eran made that life-changing trip to JH Ranch in 2010.

God used silence and solitude to prepare great leaders like Moses, Joseph, and David. The essence of who they became was contingent upon their time spent in the wilderness. This wilderness time qualified them to lead others and to discern His distinct voice apart from competing agendas. They had learned how to be in solitude with God so that when intense leadership was required, they could live firmly under His yoke no matter the conflict. None of these leaders were perfect, but they each developed priceless rituals that enriched them in wisdom and obedience and equipped them to successfully lead others.

CHAPTER 10

TRUE AUTHORITY

The Good Samaritan, "moved with compassion,"
goes into no man's land for the sake of love. He
overcomes the distinction and barriers of culture,
and through his own inward turning, he sets in
motion personal relationships.

—Ivan Illich

A mayor of Druze descent once presented Bruce and me with a framed picture of the center square of his city, featuring an ancient well and the written phrase "May the force be with you." I could tell he was swollen with pride about his city and the people he was serving. Although I didn't want to prejudge, it appeared at first glance that his religion was hooked up with the Jedi Master of *Star Wars*, Obi-Wan Kenobi.

Amid the vast sea of religions in the Middle East, the Druze community is one of the most mysterious and secretive, but those who live in Israel understand that they are excellent, hardworking citizens of Israel. This was all I needed to know about the mayor. I gave him a bear hug and thanked him profusely for his gift, as if he had given me an emerald and diamond ring.

People need to be validated and loved where they are and for who they are. They need to be able to perceive "I am with you because I feel called *by* you into friendship, called *to* you by God Himself, and yes, called to the great connection between human beings and between human beings and God." Our new Druze friend formed a partnership with us and sent hundreds of their teenagers through our biblical leadership training at the National Leadership Center. God is able to do wonder-working things when we open our hearts to those who are different than we are.

COMPASSION AT THE CORE

Compassion must be the core, and even the very nature, of authority. We have to be able to impart the compassion of God to those in our sphere of influence. Compassion occurs when I realize that other people's cravings also reside in *my* heart and that other people's sins are also rooted in *my* impulses. When others hate or cheat, I know I could have done the same. When they forgive, I know I can also forgive.[39] Compassion enables us to make sacrifices and to love human beings as sisters and brothers, whatever their status or condition.

39 | Henri Nouwen, *Wounded Healer* (New York: Doubleday Religion, 1979), 22–23.

We have all experienced what lack of compassion feels like when leaders are too political or self-serving. Leaders in all facets of life (myself included) are often so convinced of their opinions and are so confident in their personas that they believe they have a lock on truth and are right *all the time*. Perceiving that we are right and thinking that we have the inside track on truth can be so exciting and ego-inflating that it becomes increasingly more difficult to see the earth beneath our feet, and we often lose track of the people we are serving. It seems that the bigger we pump ourselves up, the easier it is to prick us with a pin.

When Jesus arrived on the scene in the first century, He was filled with compassion toward humanity. His gentleness toward sinners flowed from His divine ability to read their hearts and to see who they really were. Behind people's arrogance, airs of self-sufficiency, puzzling defense mechanisms, greed, and offenses, Jesus saw the childlike qualities in those who were before Him who had not been loved or believed in. He extracted the treasure in people whether they deserved it or not.

LOVING BEYOND BARRIERS

However, Jesus went a big step further. In His parable of the Good Samaritan, a Jewish traveler had been beaten and left for dead along the road, and an unlikely neighbor showed mercy to the injured man.[40] Jesus made the revolutionary assertion that rather than *your neighbor* only being someone from your social circle,

40 | Luke 10:25–37

your neighbor can actually be anyone. This was novel news in the first century, and it still is today. Jesus revealed that no category, custom, language, or culture defines who your neighbor is.

The relationship between the Samaritan and the beaten Jewish man is formed voluntarily, unforeseen, and outside the box. Jesus' listeners would have identified the Samaritan as the despised outsider, yet in the parable he is the hero. He travels into "fringe" territory that lies between two cultures—not to fulfill a duty, but to answer a call by God. The Samaritan was moved by compassion for the man in the ditch. When he saw him, he underwent a sudden conversion, an inward turning around that enabled him to set in motion a personal relationship with the wounded man.[41] He took him to the ER, checked him into a Holiday Inn Express, spoon-fed him some lentil soup for dinner, and then spent the night in the room next to him to make sure he was doing well in the morning.

Jesus is the Good Samaritan in the parable. For the sake of love, He repeatedly violated the proper conduct of His own society, not just through His connections with the Samaritans, but also with tax collectors, women of doubtful reputation, the insane, the dead, and so on.[42] He expanded the horizon of love for humanity and showed His talmidim that the kingdom of God stands above and beyond ethical rules, and He explained that it would likely disrupt their everyday world in completely unpredictable ways.

41 | David Cayley, *The Rivers North of the Future: The Testament of Ivan Illich* (Toronto: House of Anansi Press Inc., 2005), 31.

42 | Ibid.

Twenty years into an extraordinary relationship with the Jewish people and the nation of Israel, my heart and my horizon were further enlarged by God. I was in danger of being one-sided, caring for one people group over another. This is easy to do. I needed my vision to expand, but I must admit I did not pray for this because I did not see a need to do so. I was pretty happy inside my own fortification amid the world of people I love. That changed when I met Sheikh Ashraf Jabari.

Our Nissan sedan bounced over old cobblestones and around a winding, narrow road leading to Hebron, thirty-two kilometers south of Jerusalem. My Israeli driver, who doubled as my security guard, was concerned about going into Hebron at night, particularly Palestinian Hebron, near the ancient cave of Machpelah, where Abraham is buried next to his sons—Isaac and Ishmael—and where Sarah, Rebekah, and Jacob are also buried. I told him that he should feel very safe, that I was a professional wrestler by trade and have my black belt, although I had forgotten to bring it. He did not seem relieved at all.

Hebron is a hauntingly beautiful and ancient city, twisted and torn by decades of unrest and conflict. For the Jews, the cave of Machpelah, which is enshrouded by a fortress built by Herod in 31 BC, is one of the holiest Jewish sites, second only to the Temple Mount in Jerusalem. Having led many tours there, I was not intimidated by the surroundings, although when we arrived that evening a group of teenagers were yelling and throwing stones at each other in front of the cave. Both Israelis and Palestinians live in Hebron, but they are segregated within their own communities, with Israeli Jews being about 20 percent of the population. Traditionally, Hebron has been a source of contention between Israelis and Palestinians, and many who live there are heavily burdened by their strong conviction about who owns the land.

On this night in the spring of 2019, Sheikh Ashraf Jabari, the spiritual leader of one of the largest Palestinian families (about forty thousand people), was hosting an Iftar meal during Ramadan in his home with a large group of Israelis and Palestinians who are involved in joint business ventures. I was invited as a guest because I had been leading tours for Congress and educating them on the growing phenomenon of Israelis and Palestinians doing business together—but I had also come to Hebron with an important, yet not-so-pleasant, message for Ashraf.

Ashraf has his own militia, so when I arrived, armed soldiers were surrounding his house and neighborhood. My security guard finally felt safe. The night was surreal. I walked into the dinner party where Israeli Jews and Palestinian Muslims were laughing together over Turkish coffee, falafel, and hookah pipes. Ashraf was in the middle of everyone and was leading the conversation. I couldn't help but think how proud Father Abraham would be to see Isaac's and Ishmael's grandchildren getting along so well together. My heart melted like butter. I could see some of what God was wanting to do—He wanted to elevate the importance of integrated business in the West Bank. Most importantly that night, I felt God's love for the Palestinians in the room.

Undoubtedly, Sheikh Ashraf Jabari is a major reason why so many Palestinians and Israelis are friends today. His compassionate leadership, winsome business vision, and humble demeanor have infused life into the hearts of the Palestinian people, who long for an end to the protracted Israeli-Palestinian conflict and want to see their children prosper. After decades of anger, this generation of Palestinians is ready for a new kind of leadership and is ready to leave their low-income refugee status and enter a prosperous way of life.

Who wouldn't want that?

MODERN-DAY GOOD SAMARITAN

Like the Good Samaritan, Ashraf stepped fearlessly outside of what his culture had sanctioned for the last sixty years in order to forge new creative partnerships—a community of Jews and Muslims working together toward a prosperous economic future. Ashraf is a soft-spoken man, kindhearted and gentle. He is not what people might imagine a revolutionary to be like inside of a world-renowned conflict. He is not angry or aggressive. The present conflict requires a compassionate leader at the helm who can see into both sides and work graciously toward mutually beneficial solutions.

I waited around to break the not-so-good news to Ashraf. It was 1:30 a.m., and I was still at his house looking for the right opportunity. I could see how excited his friends and colleagues were by their recent decision to support Ashraf in forming a political party and eventually run in the presidential race against the

Palestinian Authority. However, I had received notification earlier in the day that the US administration would not support his political party or race, even behind the scenes. They believed he needed to stick with leading the business movement, which they would continue to support.

As I sat and drank a final round of tea, Ashraf looked at me in disbelief when I told him the news. He had not made a formal declaration that he was starting his own political party, but he had already raised an army of people who were ready to support him. He was calm but was clearly shaken by the news. I felt him searching my eyes for answers, but I didn't have any even though I was the one who had stood in the gap for him with the US administration.

The news was a setback for Ashraf, but I knew that our US leadership had made the right decision for the time being. Ashraf could not play both roles. He could not be a politician and also maintain a neutral leadership role in the Palestinian business community. He had to choose. That day, some of the US government leaders helped make his decision easier for him. I rode back to Jerusalem with my fearless security guard, feeling as if I had been a skunk at a wedding. I had ruined an otherwise perfect evening for Ashraf and his friends.

Over Turkish coffee the next day, Ashraf told me that he had come to a peaceful decision to remain the leader of the business movement and to forego forming the political party and running for president. He was working through the disappointment of those around him who had high hopes for a political change. I breathed a sigh of relief when I looked in his eyes and saw that he was okay.

SERVING WITH A BROKEN HEART

When our hearts are broken over the people we love and we are emptied of personal ambition, we will do anything. No sacrifice is too great. We risk everything, and we accept every disappointment while we wait patiently for a breakthrough into a new frontier. Ashraf had already put everything on the line. He and his family lived under a continuous threat from the Palestinian Authority, yet he couldn't just stop and preserve his own life. He had to continue to be the compassionate leader and to live for the sake of others, namely his countrymen who were desperate for change and the opportunity to succeed in business.

Ashraf was called to forge the future of the Palestinian people. Obviously, not everyone is a leader of a movement like he is, but Jesus' talmidim should be joined to a movement that is bringing underlying transformation to society. We can be there to strengthen, support, offer our services, volunteer, bring lemonade and cookies, and pray. We must answer the call to represent Him on Earth in our spheres of influence, and it is our job to find out how and where God wants us involved.

I AM WITH YOU

Two remarkable events followed my conversation with Ashraf at his house. During the night, Ashraf experienced a vision of Jesus wearing a white robe with gold threads standing at the end of his bed. He said to him, "Peace be upon you, My son, Ashraf. I am with you, and you are in My care. Your calling to the business community is for good, and I have come to bless you and to help you lead." Then Ashraf recounted that Jesus placed His hand on his head, and Ashraf kissed Jesus' hand. While Muslims revere Jesus as a great prophet and as the Messiah sent to guide Israel, I am not sure how often this happens to a Muslim cleric—but it probably does not happen very often.

Ashraf drove to Jerusalem to tell me in person about his encounter with Jesus. No doubt, it was a defining moment in his life. He told me he would never again doubt his leadership role and his calling to the business community. He responded to Jesus with chutzpah, as a beloved son who belonged in His house. I can't help but think this was Ashraf's "Peter" moment, where God stepped in to give him a new identity and to strengthen him for the mission.

I brought Ashraf to Capitol Hill a few months later. He shocked senior House and Senate leaders when he told them to stop supporting the Palestinian economy. As the leader of the Hebron business community, which generates 50 percent of the Palestinian GDP, Ashraf testified that the Palestinians would never be able to leave their low-income status by building a one-sided Palestinian business economy. For decades, the US had sent hundreds of millions of dollars in aid to a corrupt Palestinian Authority that produced no strong outcomes or breakthroughs with these resources—no new kindergartens or schools, no solution to the sewage problems, no new roads, no new infrastructure programs, and no new business start-ups—just a growing terror-incitement agenda against Israel that was being reinforced in the schools.

Within a year of their visit to Capitol Hill, Ashraf and his Jewish partner, Avi Zimmerman, influenced a reversal in US policy, a historic change to the law. Beginning in 2021, Congress would, for the first time, sanction investment in joint business partnerships between Palestinians and Israelis. God and His peaceful revolutionary, Sheikh Ashraf Jabari, had cleared the way for the new road ahead.

COMPELLING, SUSTAINING LOVE

Henri Nouwen said:

> *A revolutionary is not just motivated by a desire to liberate the oppressed, alleviate the poor, and end war. Their goal is not a better man, but a new man. A revolutionary is not ruled by manipulation and supported by weapons, but is ruled by love and supported by new ways of interpersonal communication. They do not think their goal will be reached in a few years or even in a few generations, but they base their commitment on the conviction it is better to give up your life than hold on to it and that the value of*

your actions does not depend on immediate results.
Revolutionaries live by a vision of a new world and
refuse to be side-tracked by trivial ambitions in
the moment.[43]

Compassion for sinners was at the root of Jesus' revolutionary authority. Through this lens, He clarified God's laws for the people and performed healing miracles. He was anticipating a new world full of redeemed people who would love each other well, where His talmidim would have such a radical commitment to love that they would change society. Their compassionate authority would be handed down to the next generation, and the next one after that.

A new command I give you, says Jesus. *Love one another. As I have loved you, so you must love one another. By this everyone will know that you are my disciples, if you love one another* (John 13:34–35). Like the Good Samaritan, this love compels you to care for the most unlikely people. Like Sheikh Ashraf Jabari, this love catapults you into your God-given identity that will impact future generations.

Undoubtedly, this was Jesus' way of thinking, and it was the way of thinking of those who perpetuated His yoke, or His interpretation of the Law. *Jesus called His twelve disciples to Him and gave them authority to drive out impure spirits and to heal every disease and sickness. . . . "As you go,"* He said, *"proclaim this message: 'The kingdom of heaven has come near. Heal the sick, raise the dead, cleanse*

43 | Nouwen, *The Wounded Healer,* 22–23.

those who have leprosy, drive out demons. Freely you have received;
freely give''' (Matthew 10:1, 7–8).

Jesus instructed His talmidim to get involved with people, to
enter the realm of the whole person, and to heal them. Like the
Good Samaritan, none of us can help anyone without becoming
involved, without entering into the painful circumstances of others, and without taking the risk of becoming hurt or even wounded
in the process.

The tragedy in our world of ambiguous relationships is that
many who seek an attentive ear or a word of support may find
that their spiritual leaders are not willing, or do not have time, to
enter into their messy lives. Is there anything more disturbing than
when the one who is supposed to be leading you is aloof to your
suffering? Loss often occurs when care is mass-produced. People
need a real human encounter with someone who is willing to listen
and who will put their faith, doubts, despair, darkness, and light
onto the table. They need help to find their way through confusion and to have an encounter with the source of life Himself—
Christ in you.

A talmid of Jesus makes God's love credible in their spheres
of influence. Compassion wipes out our self-preserving attitudes,
and it changes how we see ourselves and our place in the world. I
am convinced that God will baptize us with love for the people
we are supposed to help and serve, and it is good to ask Him for
this. Only then can we go the extra mile—or ten—with His strong,

supernatural love accompanying our efforts. When you do not know what to do or how to do it, love becomes the director, the source, and the sustainer of this mission. We come to realize that compassion for others is the most effective, influential position of all, far above earthly titles and designated roles of authority.

CHAPTER 11

OVERCOMING EVIL

We might well pray for
God to invade our lives,
for until He does we remain in peril
from a thousand foes.

—A. W. Tozer

I n a dramatic vision, like a scene out of *The Lord of the Rings*, the prophet Isaiah sees Lucifer, the leading archangel, approach the throne of God and pompously declare, *I will make myself like the Most High*.[44] Shortly thereafter, Isaiah watches as Lucifer is cast from heaven to Earth with a third of the angels.

Wait. Stop the music. Why cast Lucifer to Earth? Why not Mars or Venus? I have heard that it is pretty vacuous on those planets. Satan and his minions could have a very long time-out on chilly Mars—until Elon Musk figures out how to set up camp there for science-fiction fanatics.

44 | Isaiah 14:12–14

Think for a minute about how different your life would be if Satan wasn't roaming the earth destroying lives and making people miserable. If I had been on God's cosmic board of directors, I would have recommended anything other than sending Satan to Earth.

LUCIFER THE DECEIVER

The Bible depicts Lucifer as God's most powerful servant, responsible to no superior other than God Himself. *Lucifer* means "bringer of light," but Lucifer's glory led to his demise. He arrogantly judged God as incompetent, and he claimed himself to be the rightful ruler of the universe. Then he gathered an army of rebellious angels to storm heaven. His futile attempt to become like God secured Lucifer's identity as a deceiver and jealous counterfeiter.

In his book *The Divine Comedy*, Dante fabricates his own journey through hell, which is the realm of those who have rejected spiritual values and have yielded to their fleshly appetites of violence. The worst sin of all in Dante's hell is committing fraud against one's fellow man. The allegory represents the journey of the soul toward God through the recognition and rejection of sin.

UNDERSTANDING THE ENEMY

From the beginning of their journey with God, talmidim of Jesus need to understand the strategic ways that Satan and his emissaries operate, and they need to be able to overcome demonic influences. The apostle Paul warned us not to be ignorant of the devil's schemes, and the apostle Peter instructs us to be self-controlled and alert, firmly resisting Satan when we are embattled.[45]

Jesus required prospective talmidim to consider the battles they would enter into if they did indeed choose to be His disciples. A serious talmid takes time to prepare a battle plan for victory. If a talmid does not have a plan to overcome, there is a serious risk that he will be taken captive. Talmidim must be willing to dedicate themselves to a disciplined lifestyle in order to be effective in battle. Discipline is what leads to freedom, and there is a lot of meaning in freedom—especially in our chaotic world.

Demonic spirits are created beings that can speak to and penetrate the human soul (the mind, will, and emotions). Without an understanding of the way demons work, we do not know how to defeat them. For example, when a dark cloud of heaviness or depression pervades your life, rather than rolling up like a burrito in your down comforter and sipping tea spiced with self-pity, recognize lingering oppression for what it is—a demonic spirit—rather than simply a cloud of heaviness.

Unfortunately, people can unknowingly fall prey to a demonic spirit of depression and come into agreement with that spirit (e.g., "I'm depressed. I'm hopeless. God has abandoned me. I don't want to live.") as if they have done something to deserve these emotions—or they can stand firm and resist a demonic presence. I am not precluding physical and psychological imbalances that require a doctor, but people often have no idea that they are experiencing a

45 | 2 Corinthians 2:11 and 1 Peter 5:8

nefarious spirit (i.e., a demonic attack), and that unless they resist, agreement can easily occur.

TARGETING TALMIDIM

Evil spirits harass us in our weakest moments. They torment, deceive, compel, and defile, with a final goal to enslave and destroy us. If a demon can convince us that we are unworthy to ask or believe God for help, or if the demon can confirm our pride and reasoning or lure us into an offense with God, then the demonic spirit can successfully prevent us from experiencing God's love and power. A demonic presence allures and persuades people through their intellect and reason to idolize religious concepts that are void of a personal experience with God. Demonic spirits seek to penetrate our emotions and attitudes in order to deceive us.

There are several people who help me when I am facing spiritual warfare. One is my close friend Pam Hanes. I nicknamed her "Pearl at the Picnic" because she is a lovely, iconic Southern woman with never a hair out of place or an unkind word. She has zillions of children and grandchildren, but somehow, mysteriously, she wakes up every morning with fresh lipstick on. It is sickening because I wake up with mangled hair and no lipstick. But I tell people, "Don't be fooled by Pam's persona. She is not really 'Pearl at the Picnic.' It's a cover-up for Wonder Woman with power-packing bracelets."

Pam has a unique gift of deliverance, and she comes roaring into my house about once a month like a turbo vacuum cleaner for my emotional and spiritual life. What are friends for if not for that? She helps me detect what is going on in the spiritual realm and identify when my attitudes and emotions have slipped sideways.

Talmidim must be able to do this for each other. They must be able to expose demonic influences and render them powerless. As a rooted Presbyterian from the South, I had never heard the words "spiritual deliverance" until I was an adult. It never occurred to me that I needed to stand up to a demon. In fact, I had no real understanding of the spiritual realm at all. My view of Satan was that he reserved his red-hot hand for nightclubs, risqué parties, evil regimes, and gambling casinos. Only later in life did it occur to me: *Why would Satan and his emissaries wage war in places they've already captured?*

KNOWLEDGE IS POWER

When Bruce and I stepped into our calling as talmidim of Jesus, everything changed. Whatever pride, ignorance, reasoning, or doctrine we had held about the spiritual realm completely turned upside down. God began bringing people to train us in spiritual warfare and intercession. These people did not look like my normal array of friends. They were of a different ilk altogether. They had gained their understanding of the spiritual realm through desperation and eagerness. I quickly learned that I needed to step away from my neat and tidy controlled relationship with God and understand what Jesus meant when He told His disciples to drive out demons, particularly as it related to my personal life and family.

Jesus raised a heavenly protest against evil in all forms, especially the deceptive religious forms. He exposed evil every day, from driving the money changers out of the temple to driving demons out of people. Dealing with demons was a regular occurrence for Jesus. He revealed God's immeasurable compassion to humanity by bringing deception and evil into the light and setting people free from its power. His aim was preparing His talmidim to do the same—to effectively unravel the enemy's plans in people's lives.

LESSONS FROM JUDAS

After three years of following Jesus, Judas made it apparent in the garden of Gethsemane that none of Jesus' character had rubbed off on him. He had eaten the same humus and falafel with Jesus as His other disciples. He had heard the same teachings and had seen the same miracles. Even after being mentored under the extraordinary leadership of the Rabbi, Judas refused to submit to Him.

These facts lead to important questions: Why would God choose Judas in the first place when He knew that Judas would betray Him? Hadn't Judas made a sincere attempt to believe in Jesus? Why make a spectacle of him? What was God trying to reveal?

I don't have the answers to these questions, but I do know that I am asking the right questions. Judas's betrayal is at the very center of the most important redemptive story of human history. We need to understand why.

Maybe God wanted to expose the omnipresence of evil on Earth. Perhaps He was using Judas' betrayal to reveal the power of Satan to penetrate and influence the human heart. Jesus might have wanted us to see our own vulnerability, regardless of the notoriety and spiritual strength of the Christian groups we are connected to. Maybe God wanted us to learn through Judas that the presence of evil was at work in the circles of Jesus' dearest disciples and that Satan devises his most potent strategies where the kingdom of God is advancing.

At the epicenter of God's momentum on Earth, Satan and his demonic spirits wage war to divide and destroy passionate, wholehearted disciples. How else can we account for the number of spiritual leaders who fall into duplicitous lifestyles, hiding sexual immorality, greed, and addiction?

Consider that Peter, James, and John were deceived by demonic influences when fear and shock traumatized them as Jesus was arrested in the garden of Gethsemane. They deserted Jesus in His hour of need and ran for their lives. Yet the same disciples who fled in fear were later empowered with great boldness to advance the gospel under persecution, and they went fearlessly to their deaths for the sake of the kingdom of God.

THE GREAT ILLUSIONIST

The Evil One is a great illusionist. He is highly religious and self-righteous, and he counterfeits God's power and relationship to humanity with religion in all of its various forms. Demons exploit the truth and encourage dishonesty. They cover worthless things with glitter and seduce us away from what is real. They try to lure us into a world of delusion, unreality, and shadows. Judas clearly fell prey to the great illusionist.

It is notable, however, that even the worst atrocity inspired by the enemy is subject to God. The hellish host of religious spirits that put Jesus to death unknowingly contributed to the salvation of humankind. As Paul says, *None of the rulers of this age understood it, for if they had, they would not have crucified the Lord of glory* (1 Corinthians 2:8).

Only in a lifestyle of daily intimacy with Jesus is there a safeguard against the deception and the stronghold of the enemy. Part of Jesus' yoke was imparting authority to His disciples over evil spirits. They would have power and ability to enforce victory over demonic influence and oppression that would inevitably come against them and those they loved.

I was recently in prayer with my pit crew of friends, and I related to them that I was under an oppressive cloud. I had felt exhausted for months. I felt discouraged and hopeless, and I had a strong desire to quit working. I was burned out, and I turned my trembling self over to those in my ekklesia (community of believers) to help get to the bottom of the problem and find freedom. Using a few simple questions, my friends helped me get to the root of the issue that was troubling me: I was disappointed with God.

I had worked tirelessly for months with both the US and Israeli governments on a potentially historic breakthrough for Israel to declare sovereignty over the disputed area known as Judea and Samaria, which is where almost 80 percent of the events in the Old Testament occurred. My organization facilitated education on Capitol Hill on the positive impact this decision would have on integrated business between Palestinians and Israelis, as well as other factors. There was a two-month window of time in the summer of 2020 when this historic declaration of sovereignty could take place by the leaders of Israel.

God had impressed me to give the effort all I had, to step forward and educate Congress and the US administration on both the importance of the opportunity and the timing. I extended myself fully and was counting on success.

However, the day arrived when it became clear that the opportunity for Israel to declare sovereignty over Judea and Samaria had passed. The effort had come so close to success that I was taken by surprise when it did not work out. I had felt sure it would happen. Unfortunately, I heard the news in a manner that left me feeling as if I had been punched in the stomach.

In my shock and hurt, I couldn't separate the painful announcement from my view of God. It felt like He was the source of the disappointing news. He had sent me to do all the work, and then He left me feeling abandoned, betrayed, unprotected, cut off, confused, and humiliated. Of course, this line of thinking about God was not true, but I still bought the lie that God had abandoned me in my hour of need. During this vulnerable timeframe, the enemy presented an impressive case against

God, which I believed. Emotionally, I felt like an elevator that was headed to the basement at seventy miles per hour.

DISAPPOINTMENT WITH GOD

When there is disappointment and it feels as if God is at the center of it, it is important not to let your anger run amok. Significant disappointment does not just float away or get resolved by itself. It presses in against you in a deteriorating kind of way. Because life is full of disappointment, we need a good process for treating it.

During a meeting with my friends, I did what any angry person should do—I expressed my disappointment to God and identified the emotions I was experiencing. It went something like this: *Lord, I was cooperating with You and giving my very best like You asked me to, and now I feel betrayed and abandoned. I feel like You sent me to do an assignment even though You knew it would not succeed. Now I feel humiliated. You knew my heart. You knew that this was a soft spot for me and that I've been working on this breakthrough for Judea and Samaria for twenty years. I feel confused and unprotected by You.*

One friend very sweetly suggested that perhaps I was overly invested in the mission God had given me and that I felt overly responsible for the outcome. I thought, *Okay, hmm; I think I will punch you in the face.* Then another friend went further and said, "When things didn't work out as you had anticipated, perhaps your mind, will, and emotions took prominence over your spirit. When this happens, the enemy can take advantage of you emotionally."

I stared into space as if I had seen a pink alien—anything but look them in the eye. Words like this only widen the wound, but they were an important point of evaluation for at least one or two minutes. After that, my friends whispered something to each other and decided it was best to move on to the next phase of this friendly session.

Obviously, I did not need a set of professional counselors to coach me. I just needed some overly honest friends who love me and feel the freedom to say what they think. Next, they helped me see that my judgment toward God had brought separation between me and Him. That made sense to me. I confessed my monthlong standoff and judgment toward God. I prayed inwardly, *Lord, I judged You in my hurt and anger. I concluded that You didn't care enough about me to show me that the mission wasn't going to be successful. I made the judgment that You are not trustworthy. I decided that You did not protect me and that You allowed me to be humiliated.* After I prayed, I accepted His forgiveness and forgave the people who were involved in the incident.

My friends taught me something vitally important. Although I felt completely justified in my argument, it is not really ever appropriate to stay offended with God. He happens to never be wrong, which we discover in the story of Job, who argued with God for thirty-six long chapters. The falsehood that God would betray or abandon us is a trapdoor leading to captivity, and I had clearly fallen through and was under a depressive cloud.

One of my friends told me to go back and reflect on the disappointing announcement, but this time to envision God speaking to me about a job well done. I thought about what He might be saying: *Heather, you have been faithful in every step I have given you. I am proud of you. I am governing the process, and the timing will come for Israel to make a declaration of sovereignty. You are living in My great favor.*

Something snapped inside of me. Over the next day or so, I felt like I had made a comeback. When my spirit submitted to God's love for me and to His unchanging nature, I was free. By relinquishing my arguments against Him and disagreeing with a lie, I quickly emerged from fog and fatigue.

Some people might say that this is a bunch of hocus pocus: "Don't try to tell me that demonic spirits are around every corner trying to capture you." But the insider truth is that they are. Paul said that our real struggle in this life *is not against flesh and blood—* the horrible boss, the arrogant father, or the rebellious child—*but against the rulers, against the authorities, against the powers of this dark world and against the spiritual forces of evil in the heavenly realms* (Ephesians 6:12).

PLAN, PRACTICE, AND GOD'S PEOPLE

A talmid of Jesus needs a reliable plan—a daily practice and rhythm that prepares them for battle. Jesus relied on the promises of God when He faced an intense cosmic battle with Satan in the wilderness. He literally used Scripture to refute Satan and to render his temptations and oppression invalid. Jesus won the battle through His trust in the promises of God. These promises reveal where our victory lies and give us a platform to cooperate with God to enforce victory. The talmidim of Jesus had this to say: *Lord, even the demons submit to us in your name.* Jesus responded, *I have given you authority to trample on snakes and scorpions and to overcome all the power of the enemy; nothing will harm you* (Luke 10:17, 19).

We also see an important pattern in the early ekklesia, who gathered together on a regular basis in the first century. Their commitment to God and to each other safeguarded them in the presence of evil and persecution and enabled the manifest presence of God to operate in His fullest measure.

I am joined to an ekklesia of men and women who spend a lot of time together. Some of us have been together for more than twenty years. We gather on phone calls and in homes to pray and take communion. We share our breakthroughs and sorrows. We pray for Israel, and we give testimonies of the miracles that we experience. We have followed the model of the early ekklesia of the first century who came together around a common goal and who made sacrifices for one another and the mission.

These relationships are the vibrant lifeline that keeps us inside the kingdom of God and keeps us advancing His plans and agendas. This pit crew of friends has made significant contributions in transforming society, both in the United States and in the nation of Israel. We have overcome extraordinary warfare together, and we have developed a reliable shield that works amid the storms of life. We overcome Satan's emissaries when we are provoked, not unlike the early church did—*by the blood of the Lamb, and by the word of their testimony; and they loved not their lives unto the death* (Revelation 12:11 KJV).

THE PRESENCE OF GOD

There is no substitute for the presence of God in our pursuit to live victoriously. I roll my eyes when I hear religious people say, "You don't need an experience with God in order to obey Him. Don't seek experiences; that's emotionalism. Don't seek gifts; seek the Giver. You don't have to feel God and have encounters with Him; just obey His Word." This may sound like good theology, but it really isn't. The ekklesia of the first century showed us the opposite.

Disciples need the manifest presence of God for their spiritual life in order to work with Him and for Him. This includes experiences of hearing the Holy Spirit speak to us. We *do* need to feel and experience Him! The Holy Spirit has the ability to penetrate every seeking heart and to intermingle with our human spirit. Moral evil is forced to withdraw. God's presence is life itself, the infusion of energy, the breeze that brings dead places back to life within us. His presence renews our mind to what is true.

We should not abandon what made the early talmidim so successful. Only by sticking together could they keep bouncing back in the midst of loss and disappointment. Their zeal for God, their dedication to stay at one with Him, and their resolve to work and pray together became both their protection against the enemy and their strategy for advancing the kingdom of God.

CHAPTER 12

ADVANCING

I believe we should profit immensely were we to declare a period of silence and self-examination during which each one of us searched his own heart and sought to meet every condition for a real baptism of power from on high.

—A. W. Tozer

Although humans have historically exhausted themselves trying to prove that we are the "masters of our fate" and "captains of our soul," we are not the Higher Power. We forget the wisdom of the old riddle: "What's the difference between you and God? God never thinks He's you."

Interestingly, when we partner in His larger cause, we become redirected, refocused, and rescued from our personal fixations. We hook into the bigger things that God is doing in the world, and in that redemptive process, we find ourselves. We see and

understand our true identity up against the larger picture of who
we were created to be.

The early talmidim were successful at this transformational
process. They put the kingdom of God first and facilitated God's
redemptive plans in the lives of people—and in the process, they
found who they were. They took care of what was important to
God, and He took care of what was important to them. But how
do we as modern disciples really advance His kingdom?

INFUSION OF POWER

I believe that the key to advancing God's kingdom is friendship
with God. It really is that simple, which is why Jesus insisted on
His talmidim taking the necessary time to prepare themselves for
a real baptism of power from on high—an invasion of God's Spirit
into their personal lives. The Holy Spirit would take the prominent place as their direct link to the Godhead. In Acts 1:8, when
Jesus says to His talmidim, *You will receive power*, He is promising
them intimacy with God that will be supernatural. Jesus knows
that only this penetration of power from above will make spiritual
things real to the souls of His disciples and will enable them to
experience the piercing closeness of His love.

When the Holy Spirit has come upon us with His power, our
conversation with God loses its dry and routine quality, becoming instead an intimate dialogue with Someone who is actually
there. In fact, it is a conversation with One who is captivatingly

near. Only with a genuine infusion of power can love for God and others take possession of us.

The New Testament speaks of this power as the ability to do, or to act. The Holy Spirit was never viewed by Jesus' talmidim as a luxury item given to a few people to produce an exclusive type of Christian. No—He was the vital necessity, the inescapable imperative for every talmid and their ability to cooperate with God.

Only the Holy Spirit can win our hearts over in obedience to the whole will of God. We desperately need His divine power in order to advance His kingdom. Jesus' talmidim were not sent to a catechism class to get a grip on the proper doctrine to spread to the world, but they were sent first to do one thing only: they were to wait in Jerusalem until they had been clothed with power from on high.[46]

Talmidim of Jesus must take this priority so seriously that they arrange their lives around very personal encounters with the Holy Spirit. I do not know of a specific formula that can lead a person into this encounter. The most important ingredient is to make the shift so that the Holy Spirit is given prominence and becomes your closest companion. Every serious talmid of Jesus continually takes time away from the world to abandon themselves in worship and to entreat the Holy Spirit. There is a certain desperation that is absolutely necessary—the pouring out of one's self in absolute surrender and worship of Him. The Holy Spirit goes where He is longed for and wanted. Once the Holy Spirit initially comes with

46 | Luke 24:49

power into your life, you will know it. Then He comes again and again. The first encounter with Him is vital, and it opens the way for encounter after encounter with Him as a way of life.

This leads us back to chutzpah, a raw-nerve appeal to God, seen in the men who ripped open the roof to get their paralyzed friend to Jesus, the hemorrhaging woman who lunged for Jesus' robe, the blind man who shouted obnoxiously to Jesus from the roadside, and the centurion who imagined Jesus healing his servant without needing to lay eyes on him. The people in each of these stories were not only healed, but they were also praised for their audacious faith.

In the same way, the Holy Spirit comes with power into our lives through our faith-filled appeals. Will not God give the Holy Spirit to those who ask Him? *For everyone who asks receives; the one who seeks finds; and to the one who knocks, the door will be opened* (Luke 11:10, 13).

AUTHENTIC FRUIT

There is a special quality of fruit that comes from the life of a talmid who is wholly surrendered to the Holy Spirit. In writing about a defining event called judgment day, the apostle Paul tells us that we will encounter the results of the way we lived on Earth, and that the fruit of our life will determine what eternity in heaven will be like for us when we get there.[47]

Several of my friends are interior designers, and my sister is a talented furniture designer. One of the fastest ways to disgust a

47 | 1 Corinthians 3:11–15

Southern designer is to have artificial flowers in your home. That is a real no-no. Nevertheless, I am one of those who tries to cheat the system. Due to my travel schedule and my habit of killing plants stone dead, I have several artificial orchids in prominent places in my house. You would have to come close and touch them to realize they are fake, but for the sake of my social circle, which is filled with experts, I mix real plants in to make the orchids look more real. I get by—sort of.

The notion that my life on Earth will culminate in a rewards banquet where Jesus will judge the real versus the artificial fruit in my life has always kind of bothered me. It is hard to imagine how this is going to work, not to mention that people's feelings could be hurt. I have often wondered if God gives an "investment for eternity" advantage to some people more than to others. For instance, did He give more life-investment potential to Billy Graham and to Abraham than to the devout disciple who was crippled and lived on the support of others while on Earth? Will the rewards banquet be drastically different for Billy Graham? What about the mom at home with her four children versus the father who goes to work and has the opportunity to invest in thirty employees every day?

I think God wants us to understand that the small things we do during the course of a day are extremely important to Him and hold the same fruit-bearing value as what we view to be the "larger picture" efforts. The young prophet Samuel told the corrupted priest Eli that the things of greatest importance to God are often the small, hidden things we do with steady obedience in the right direction. Samuel reminded the misguided King Saul, *Does the Lord delight in burnt offerings and sacrifices as much as in obeying the Lord? To obey is better than sacrifice, and to heed is better than the fat of rams* (1 Samuel 15:22).

I imagine that heaven's reward ceremony will be very different from anything we have ever experienced. Whether one is cleaning a house or preaching in a stadium, Jesus said that authentic fruit is the result of intimately abiding in Him. This is why I think this reward day will be full of surprises. God rewards authentic fruit. It stands to reason that some of the seemingly most insignificant people in society may be exalted on that day, and some of the most powerful may be humbled. The Nobel Prizes of Heaven may go to unlikely characters. People will receive rewards for what they have done because of their friendship with Him.

In His parables, Jesus spoke about rewards in terms of being given certain levels of responsibility in heaven that correspond to one's faithful deeds on the earth.[48] I know that all of this sounds very ethereal, but I have arranged my life around the important understanding that every day counts, and that if we are not paying attention, we could wake up one day with deep regret.

Talmidim live fruitful lives empowered by the Holy Spirit, and they pause to find out where to invest their time. They join Him to see breakthroughs occur—for people and for society, which includes justice for the oppressed, as well as changed laws and policies. This is why His talmidim are often sent into secular

48 | Matthew 25:14–30

spheres. They are joined together with those who are transforming society. They live fruitful lives of love that will most assuredly outlast them.

THE INSIDE SCOOP

After many years of seeing answered prayers, Bruce and I no longer pray in the same way that we did in our earlier days. We now believe that God reveals His plans and invites us to believe Him in advance, even if a lot of the details are unknown or seem impossible through human eyes. Our expectation that He will do the impossible has the potential to make us look a little crazy to others, so we keep a lot of our expectations to ourselves. No wonder Jesus told His talmidim to go into their closets to pray.[49] He was giving them a heads-up that we will look crazy if we bring all of our faith-filled expectations out into the open.

God responds to a hidden life of prayer that packs a punch, and the only way this happens is if we have some idea of what we are supposed to be praying, along with some notion of what His plans are in advance. This is why one of the expectations Jesus set forth in relation to the Holy Spirit was that He would show them things yet to come.[50] They would receive the inside scoop about what He wanted to accomplish in given situations that required their prayers.

Bruce and I pray for our children. We pray about our finances.

49 | Matthew 6:6

50 | John 16:13

We pray for our extended family. We pray often. However, we listen more than we pray so that we can discern what God wants us to do. What we hear changes the dynamic of how we pray. We both need a lot from God in order for life to work well, but we never take our eyes off the ball of what He is doing in the wider world—and we don't stop giving ourselves wholly to what is important to Him.

THE KING'S HIGHWAY

I envision this process to be like a highway, the King's Highway, which is the movement of God on Earth to transform societies all over the world. To be on the King's Highway every day is to care about what He cares about in the larger sense of the kingdom of heaven. It can seem extraneous to care about the bigger picture when you are struggling with ten other problems in your personal life, or are not married yet, or haven't been able to land a job, or haven't been able to have a baby, etc.

If we rely on our human capacity, this is nearly impossible. Our soul—mind, will, and emotions—is finite and limited. We just don't have the bandwidth for that kind of emotional multi-tasking. It is possible, though, through His Spirit pouring into our spirit. The more time we spend listening to Him, the greater our ability is to hear and respond to the Spirit regarding the world's problems despite our own difficulties.

Talmidim get out of balance quickly when they turn inward and center their prayers continuously around their own needs and lack. We get stuck when we do that. An overarching guideline for a talmid is "Don't get off the King's Highway and onto a dirt road of your own making." Your wheels will get stuck in the mud. We must keep the agenda of the King's Highway front and center when we bring our needs to Him.

Somehow when we are prayerful about His agenda—for example, whether it is about seeing human trafficking come to an end in our nation, or watching biblical prophecies about Israel come into fullness, or a deadly pandemic coming to an end, and so on— we find ourselves more centered in the universe. When we operate from the soul, our gaze tends to remain inward—on spiritual lockdown. But when we function in His Spirit, He turns our attention outward to focus on the larger world.

Eran Glazer, who heard the Lord speak to him on top of the Leap of Faith at JH Ranch and who became the director of Israel's National Leadership Center, is facilitating a cultural shift that is taking place inside the State of Israel today. Most of the world is not privy to it because the changes are taking place deep inside Israeli society and in their major educational venues, but this shift inside their culture is very significant and was anticipated by God Himself.

Eran hikes to the top of the mountain above the National Leadership Center every day and stretches out his hands in prayer over the nation. Sometimes he feels strong and full of faith, and other times he feels a little wobbly. I pray the same kind of prayers from Alabama with my group of friends. Our prayers are centered around a new generation of Israelis being able to relate to God more personally and being willing to open their hearts to Him. I realize that most people don't do this kind of thing. Most people do not pray outside their cultural lines or into some large and looming, hard-to-nail-down agenda. It can seem that prayers like this are outside of reality and are irrelevant to what is directly in your neighborhood. We would rather pray and care about things that give back to us in some way.

However, there is something altogether different about prayers that represent the Father's heart for a nation. He said that His house would be *a house of prayer for all nations*, which means that to be connected to a larger national or international purpose is to be hooked into His reality and priority.[51] I have watched God answer our prayers over the nation of Israel. We ask. He responds. Sometimes it takes longer than I want, but He delivers.

I believe this happens across the gamut of society for talmidim everywhere, whether they are involved in a business merger that impacts the quality of a nation, political agendas that reflect godly policy, or justice that needs to advance inside of cultures. Talmidim of Jesus take part in transforming society, and they gravitate to others who can join in a similar vision. I am convinced this is how God gets His best work done on Earth.

A few years ago, the Lord awoke me each night for a period of time into a vision of Ezekiel 36:26: *I will give you a new heart and put a new spirit in you; I will remove from you your heart of stone and*

51 | Isaiah 56:7

give you a heart of flesh. He showed me a future international prayer movement being established for the nation of Israel with many different kinds of people and nations involved, and He helped me understand the spiritual shift the nation of Israel would undergo in fulfillment of this prophecy from Ezekiel 36. This three-thousand-year-old prophecy would not come to pass in a vacuum or be a sign to the nation of Israel alone, but it would be the sign of all nations turning to Him, with Israel being the catalyst. I understood that God was up to something, but I couldn't see how this would play out.

Eran awoke one night during the same time frame, but his encounter with God was much more dramatic. He experienced a vision of the wild prophet Elijah at the end of his bed. It was sensational to say the least. Eran called me the following day, terrified about what he had seen. I listened intently. He heard the words: "Prepare the way of the Lord. Lift up the road for God. I am taking out the heart of stone and giving Israel a heart of flesh. I am putting a new spirit inside the nation. I want you to raise up an international prayer movement for the nation of Israel."

I could almost feel Eran trembling on the other side of the phone. What normal person receives a message from Elijah the prophet in the middle of the night? The vision was disruptive, startling, and unforgettable. We were on opposite sides of the world, yet we had each dramatically heard the same words within the same week.

Neither of us were related to the right people who could help us accomplish this task. I spent the better part of the phone call calming Eran down and explaining to him that I had heard almost the same thing that he had heard and seen. The truth is that I too was taken aback by the whole scenario. Where do we go from here? Both of us were so busy. How do we even take a first step? After several conversations, we prayed a simple prayer that God would show us the way forward to develop an international prayer movement for Israel. We never prayed about it again.

I realize that this situation sounds like something that would only happen to a few select people, but that is not true. Whether with a business partner, a spouse, a loyal coworker, or a close political ally, God works in unique ways with His talmidim to bring people together to advance His kingdom. He speaks to them in very different ways. He does not need to speak through visions for you to know that you are supposed to surrender to an impossible task.

God gives sufficient signs along the way to validate bold steps of faith. He joins our faith, whether over a business merger, a sum of money that you are being asked to give that is beyond anything you have given before, or a partnership you are to form with someone you don't know very well. He brings disparate people together to advance His kingdom agenda.

Shortly after these events, I received a call from Musette Morgan, one of my closest friends, who has been in lockstep with me in starting two organizations related to Israel. As a best friend is supposed to do, she helps me quit my job about once a year in my moments of despair, and then she helps me reemploy myself again and stay with it. She called to encourage me to get in touch with Lou Engle, the founder of a ministry called The Send. She sensed he would be an important factor in helping us start the prayer movement for Israel. If you have a helpful group of friends, it is good to listen to them. We want simple answers to complex problems, but rather than give you answers, God oftentimes sends you friends to help you iron out your next steps.

I did not know Lou Engle, except that he is known as a man of prayer and has tens of thousands of intercessors connected to his network. As a first step, I decided to call a few of his friends. They reached out to Lou for me, but he did not respond. This went on for months. I made phone calls, sent smoke signals, and then arranged for a drone attack. Nothing worked. Finally, I ended up at a conference and realized that Lou Engle was there, but I was sort of miffed that he had not responded to my calls.

I went to my hotel room, and the Lord rearranged my thinking. He deeply impressed on my heart that Lou would help lead the prayer movement for the nation of Israel. He would be like Simeon in the early days of Jesus—a man who understood the season of Israel's restoration.[52] I heard the Lord say to me that Lou would play a dynamic leadership role in building a prayer movement for Israel from around the world, adding to the efforts of others who have plowed in this field.

52 | Luke 2:25–35

I realized how silly I was to try to get on a phone call with him to explain something that was so serious to God. We needed a face-to-face meeting. For the first time, I got a picture of the serious nature of what we were embarking upon, realizing that it would have financial, governmental, and spiritual implications for the nation of Israel. The next morning, I found myself standing in line at Starbucks behind Lou's wife, Therese. We introduced ourselves, and once she realized who I was, she invited me to sit and have coffee with them. Lou had been on an extended fast and had grown a beard, and he looked like a wild prophet. I thought about Eran's vision.

We exchanged niceties, and I told Lou what Eran and I had heard from the Lord. He said that the Lord had shown him some of the very same things. After several hours of conversation, he said he would like to spend the remaining days of his fast in Israel, so I arranged for him to stay in our condominium in the city of Ariel. Within a matter of a few weeks, both of us were in Israel with part of his team.

Lou hiked around the National Leadership Center, where he met Eran Glazer. Eran was a little afraid of Lou because he rocked back and forth when he prayed and had a bolder way of communicating than Eran had ever experienced. But he got the courage and he asked Lou to climb the Leap of Faith, and Lou agreed. As Lou was climbing the pole, Eran told him to jump out to the trapeze, telling him that he was taking a giant leap into a new season where he would have a dramatic impact on the nation of Israel. It was a surreal, breathtaking meeting that day where the three of us, very different people, merged together to find a way forward to raise up a prayer movement for Israel.

Several years have passed since that day, and tens of thousands of people from around the world are now engaging in intercession for the nation of Israel in the areas of government, education, and business. This host of intercessors is fervently praying for the prophesied cultural and spiritual shift in Israel whereby God will remove the heart of stone and give a heart of flesh and a new spirit to the people. An international prayer movement started because groups of disparate people agreed to join each other to see it happen, even if some of us were weak-kneed about it.

God cooperates with His risk-taking friends. He typically does not work out His plans in a safe and comfortable way but rather on the edge, where we are helpless and have to rely on different personalities for His kingdom to advance. We take nervy steps of faith around what He is revealing, whether in business, in politics, or at home—but God does the heavy lifting of changing hearts and bringing relationships together. It is only in this place that we can witness God perform the impossible.

In a dynamic friendship with us, the Holy Spirit leads us out to the edge of things to take risks for the sake of love. Each risk is important to Him and is linked to eternal fruit. He chooses to speak to each one of His talmidim in real time, uniquely and personally. A talmid has an authentic prayer life and an active friendship with God because the Holy Spirit penetrates their heart and transforms their thinking to enable them to follow Him with supernatural love into a world that is thirsting for Him.

CONCLUSION

As you come to the end of this book, my hope is that you have reached an ultimate and central decision to become a talmid of Jesus. It might seem like a dose of folly at first to make this mad exchange of everything you have for the identity of a talmid. However, once you comprehend that God wildly loves you and gave up everything just for you, then you fall facedown in adoration, lost in wonder and praise.

Suddenly, there is no sacrifice too great. It becomes easier than you thought to make the bold decision to trust God deeply for a lifetime, knowing that never in a million years could you out-give, outmatch, or outdo what He will achieve in and through you. After long periods of personal introspection over the nagging question "Who am I?" Rabbi Jesus gave me light to see. His love-impelled invasion into my life changed everything, including my intimacy with God, my relationships with others, my care for Israel, and my gentleness toward myself.

Still, to be a talmid of Jesus requires a heavy dose of chutzpah—courageous decision-making and risk-taking resolve. It requires a life of listening and following Him in real time. Jesus singled out and summoned His disciples. He told them to sell their lucrative fields and buy the kingdom pearl of great price—and He told them not to look back for one moment. He made no apologies for any personal losses they might incur, because it was simply not worth mentioning in view of the life He was offering them.

When we realize God's great love for humanity, we come into our own self-acceptance and are able to treat others with the same unconditional honor and reverence. When we turn away from self-incrimination, we can hook into His plans for transforming society and can get off the side road of preoccupation with our needy personal lives. Time and again, talmidim move through ominous feelings of helplessness and into a nervy faith for the impossible. This is how the kingdom of God is brokered in a talmid's sphere of influence. They facilitate the presence of God on Earth.

The real wonder of life is found when Jesus places His restful, supernatural yoke upon us. When Jesus said, *Come to me, all you who are weary and burdened,* He understood that we would grow weary, discouraged, and disappointed along the way.[53] He did not paint any romantic pictures, yet His original talmidim left behind their sinful lives to follow Him because His yoke brought freedom—not only for themselves, but also for others. They wanted to exchange their insignificant lives for something exponentially greater. They set their sights on becoming like the Rabbi, and indeed they became like Him.

53 | Matthew 11:28

ACKNOWLEDGMENTS

Uncommon Favor: The Intentional Life of a Disciple represents a lifetime of support and strength from many valiant people. My first and foremost thanks to Bruce, who has been my lover, companion, and champion. I would be nowhere without you, especially when it comes to outlandish adventure.

My parents, David and Gloria Hampe, and Bruce's parents, Gene and Joy Johnston, have modeled genuine godly lives that have been worthy of emulating, and we have drawn deeply from each of their unique characters.

My mentor and spiritual father, Dr. James Houston, has played the strong, influential, spiritual role in my life. Like a rabbi, he has helped me find my true self and to risk everything. My close friend, Pam Hanes, has lived ahead of me, has shown me what sacrificial love for others is like, and has been a constant source of strength.

Joan Leslie McGill, Allison Smith, Musette Morgan, Shelly Beach, and Kyle Duncan spent hours and days reading the manuscript and offered valuable insights and edits. No doubt their enthusiastic encouragement undergirded my steps. I could not have written this book without them. John Riddle's invaluable insights on listening and hearing from God and Bill Johnson's influence on my understanding of the kingdom of heaven are threads throughout this book.

And to my pit crew of friends, intercessors, JH Israel and USIEA staff and Board of Directors, you have made life worth living. You have audaciously dropped your nets, set out into the unknown, and have sacrificially given everything you have. You have pioneered valiantly and continue to do so. I would not want to be on this journey without you.

ADDITIONAL RESOURCES

JH Israel website: jhisrael.com

JH Ranch website: jhranch.com

US Israel Education Association website: usieducation.org

JH Outback website: jhoutback.com